Brent Davis Reid

Parallels

EXPLORING THE ISSUES

Get Connected ...

Explore ...

Succeed!

Parallels: Exploring the Issues Companion Website

www.longmanesl.ca/reid.cw

Forty-four additional exercises and related links to promote English proficiency:

✔ **Reading, listening, writing and speaking activities related to subjects covered in** *Parallels: Exploring the Issues*

✔ **Varied exercise types: automatic correction with formative feedback** *and* **self-corrected short answers**

✔ **Vocabulary enrichment exercises**

✔ **Alternative writing projects**

✔ **Individual and paired speaking projects**

Tailor-made for you by the author of *Parallels: Exploring the Issues*

To access
the Companion Website

Step 1 Go to **www.longmanesl.ca/reid.cw**

Step 2 Choose **Parallels: Exploring the Issues**.

Step 3 When asked, enter the following username and password:

| **Username** | cw20030 | **Password** | bc98bf |

Step 4 Follow the instructions on the screen.

Note to Teachers
To obtain a username and password that will allow you to access the Teacher Section of the Companion Website, please contact your Pearson Longman ESL consultant.

Technical Support: tech@erpi.com

W-32617

Brent Davis Reid

Parallels

EXPLORING THE ISSUES

PEARSON
Longman

DISTRIBUTED IN CANADA BY ERPI
5757, RUE CYPIHOT, SAINT-LAURENT (QUÉBEC) H4S 1R3
TELEPHONE: 514 334-2690 ext. 232   FAX: 514 334-0448
infoesl@erpi.com   www.longmanesl.ca

ACKNOWLEDGEMENTS

Many thanks to those involved in the project:

- Lucie Turcotte for her insight and patience
- Sharnee Chait for her continued guidance
- The ERPI team for their *unparalleled* professionalism
- Friends and family for "cheering me on"
- The following colleagues who provided feedback:
  Cecilia Delgado (Collège Lionel-Groulx)
  Étienne Guay (Cégep de Trois-Rivières)
  Chiara Laricchiuta (Collège Ahuntsic)
  Mary Jean Martin (Collège François-Xavier-Garneau)
  Susan Meier (Cégep régional de Lanaudière)
  Suzanne Pichard (Cégep de Sainte-Foy)
  Brenda Young (Collège François-Xavier-Garneau)

In memory of B.

Managing Editor
Sharnee Chait

Editor
Lucie Turcotte

Copy Editor
My-Trang Nguyen

Proofreader
Katie Shafley

Permissions
Marie-Chantal Masson

Art Director
Hélène Cousineau

Graphic Design Coordinator
Karole Bourgon

Book Design
Dessine-moi un mouton
Sylvie Morissette

Cover Design
Sylvie Morissette

Page Layout
Talisman illustration design

Illustrations
Rémy Guenin   pp. 4, 9, 26, 53, 57, 68, 73, 84, 89, 96, 98, 99, 103, 114, 119, 124, 129, 134, 139, 145, 150, 160, 166
Anne Villeneuve   pp. 1, 15, 19, 49, 81, 110, 141

CREDITS

Unit 1, p. 9 Audio text "In People We Trust" by Terry Mosher © Canadian Broadcasting Corporation.

Unit 2, p. 20 Photograph of gun © Jupiterimages. p. 22 "Not Again!" cartoon by Aislin, reprinted by permission of Terry Mosher. p. 23 "Strengthen Gun Laws" originally published in the *Barrie Examiner*, September 25, 2006; reprinted by permission of James Mennie and *The Gazette*. p. 26 Video segments "Anastasia's Law" and "Gun Registry in Rural Canada" © CTV. p. 34 "Global Warming" photograph © digitalife / Shutterstock. p. 37 "Variation of the Earth's Surface Temperature for the Past 1000 years © IPCC. p. 37 "Myths from Skeptics Slowing Us Down" by David Suzuki, originally published in the *Owen Sound Sun Times*, May 25, 2007; reprinted by permission of the David Suzuki Foundation (www.davidsuzuki.org). p. 41 Video segments "Melting Arctic Sea Ice," Part I and Part 2 © CTV. p. 41 Photographs of the Arctic sea ice © PUBLIPHOTO / SPL / NASA.

Unit 3, p. 50 Photograph of roulette © Sebastian Duda / Shutterstock. pp. 53-54 "Bad Poker Night Curbed My Enthusiasm" by Brian Williams, published in *The Guelph Mercury*, December 1, 2006; reprinted by permission of *The Guelph Mercury*. p. 57 Video segments "Gambling and Suicide" and "Teen Gambling Addiction" © CTV. p. 66 Photograph of cosmetic surgery © iStockphoto. pp. 69-70 "Waiting a Lifetime for Plastic Surgery" by Ashley Bursey, originally published in the *New Brunswick Telegraph Journal*, March 31, 2007; reprinted by permission of the *New Brunswick Telegraph Journal*, a CanWest partnership. p. 72 Audio texts "Fountain of Youth," Part 1 and Part 2 © Canadian Broadcasting Corporation.

Unit 4, p. 51 Photograph of bicycle © PHOTOCREO Michal Bednarek / Shutterstock. p. 85 "Living Your Life without Worry" by Susan Semanak, originally published in the *Times Colonist* (Victoria), August 22, 2005; reprinted by permission of CanWest News Service, a CanWest partnership. p. 89 Audio text "Interview with Issa" © Canadian Broadcasting Corporation. p. 95 Photograph of sandwich © Rene Jansa / Shutterstock. pp. 99-100 "Pass the Celery: I'm Seventy but My Heart's Only Fifty-five" by Jim Salter, originally published in *The Hamilton Spectator*, January 14, 2006; reprinted by permission of The Associated Press © 2008. All rights reserved. p. 103 Video segments "Caloric Restriction Diet Study," Part 1 and Part 2 © CTV.

Unit 5, p. 111 Photograph of girl with cellphone © Rich Legg / iStockphoto. pp. 115-116 "Do Phones Have a Role in School?" by Siobhan Bradley reprinted by permission of the author. p. 118 Video segments "Teen Drivers Using Cellphones," Part 1 and Part 2 © CTV. p. 126 Photograph of dna double helix © Falko Matte / Shutterstock. pp. 130-131 "'Culture of Perfection' Destroying Us" by Helen Henderson, originally published in *The Toronto Star*, September 8, 2007; reprinted by permission of Torstar Syndication Services. p. 133 Video segment "Female Feticide" © Canadian Broadcasting Corporation.

Unit 6, p. 142 Photograph of surveillance camera © sculpies / Shutterstock. pp. 146-147 "Exploding Pants Might Give Terrorists Ideas" by Les MacPherson, originally published in *The StarPhoenix* (Saskatoon); reprinted by permission of *The StarPhoenix* (Saskatoon), a CanWest partnership. p. 149 Video segment "The List" © Canadian Broadcasting Corporation. p. 157 Photograph of syringe © iStockphoto. p. 161-163 "Twelve Hours Later I Couldn't Raise My Legs—Polio Nightmare Lingers" by Gifford Jones, originally published in *The Sault Star*, July 30, 2005; reprinted by permission of the author. p. 165 Video segments "HPV Vaccination for Young Women" and "Vaccinating Young Children against Influenza" © CTV.

Additional Reading p. 173 "If I Did Wrong, the Other Person Was at Fault, Okay?" by Lisa Fitterman, originally published in *The Vancouver Sun*, February 5, 2007; reprinted by permission of the author. p. 174 "Youth Gambling a Growing Concern" by Paul Barton, originally published in *The North Bay Nugget*, May 9, 2006; reprinted by permission of Sun Media Corp. p. 175 "Eating Fewer Calories Could Lead to Longer Life" by Lindsey Tanner, originally published in *The Standard* (St. Catharines), April 5, 2006; reprinted by permission of the Associated Press © 2008. All rights reserved. p. 176 "On the Road" by Andrea Macko, originally published in *St. Marys Journal Argus*, April 2, 2008; reprinted by permission of the author. p. 177 "I'm Sick as a Dog—Literally" by Don Braid, originally published in the *Calgary Herald*, November 30, 2003; reprinted by permission of Calgary Herald Group Inc., a CanWest partnership.

Photograph "Be Heard" (detail), front cover, pp. 13, 30, 45, 61, 76, 92, 106, 122, 137, 153, 169 © iStockphoto.

Photograph "Bee at Work" (detail), pp. 2, 21, 35, 51, 67, 83, 97, 112, 127, 143, 158 © Sándor F. Szabó / iStockphoto.

Photograph "Duet of the Puffins," front cover, pp. 17, 32, 47, 63, 79, 94, 108, 124, 139, 155, 172 © Scott Hunt / iStockphoto.

Photograph "Good News" (detail), pp. 9, 26, 41, 57, 72, 89, 103, 118, 133, 149, 165 © Cristian Ardelean / iStockphoto.

Photograph of files in filing cabinet, pp. 2, 20, 34, 50, 66, 82, 95, 111, 126, 142, 157 © Dariusz Sas / Shutterstock.

Photograph of open book, front cover, pp. 4, 22, 36, 52, 68, 84, 98, 114, 129, 144, 159 © zimmytws / Shutterstock.

Photograph of *go* word, front cover, pp. 16, 31, 46, 62, 77, 93, 107, 123, 138, 154, 170 © kd2 / Shutterstock.

Photograph of pencils, front cover, pp. 12, 29, 44, 60, 75, 91, 106, 121, 136, 152, 168 © Photothèque ERPI

Parallels: Exploring the Issues is a comprehensive four-skill textbook aimed at low intermediate to intermediate students of English as a Second Language (ESL) studying science and the humanities.

There are six units in the textbook. It is strongly recommended that everyone start at the beginning, which introduces the notions of "right" and "wrong"—key concepts throughout the text. Units 2–6 are each divided into two sections: Section A is intended for humanities students; Section B, for science students. Many sections are appropriate to either field of study and may be completed in any order deemed appropriate.

The title—*Parallels: Exploring the Issues*—is significant because:

- Selected Canadian articles, as well as radio and television segments, *parallel* the students' fields of study, focusing on program-related vocabulary.
- Regardless of their programs, students have *parallel* learning experiences in that they are asked to accomplish similar tasks in *parallel* sections.
- The accompanying eleven-unit grammar workbook (*Parallels: Exploring the Issues English Grammar*) *parallels* the topics covered in the eleven sections of this textbook.

The subtitle, *Exploring the Issues*, highlights the many controversial and challenging topics examined in the textbook: personal morality, gun control, global warming, gambling, cosmetic surgery, voluntary simplicity, restricted caloric diets, juvenile cellphone usage, eugenics, public security and mandatory vaccination.

Throughout the book, students are given strategies to assist written and oral comprehension as well as written and oral production. Notes relating to commonly used expressions are included in order to enrich cultural awareness. Finally, because no one is an island unto himself (or herself), paired speaking and writing projects, as well as paired vocabulary review activities, are located at the end of each unit.

To finish, there is considerable similarity between *Parallels: Exploring the Issues* and its upper-intermediate predecessor, *Parallels: Taking a Stand in English*. This similarity is intentional: college ESL students, regardless of their language ability, merit qualitatively similar learning experiences that challenge them to communicate thoughts and feelings clearly and effectively with others who may, or may not, share their sentiments. It is hoped this sharing will occur in a welcoming atmosphere where divergent opinions are not only tolerated, but wholly accepted.

Warmest regards,

Brent Davis Reid
Montreal, January 2008

HIGHLIGHTS

Provides topic backgrounder from a Canadian perspective.

Warm-up activities generate student interest and tap into students' prior knowledge.

Each unit includes learning strategies to improve reading and listening.

Students learn about the origins of words and expressions.

Authentic audio texts from CBC radio and video segments from CBC television and CTV develop students' listening skills with vocabulary and comprehension activities.

Contains suggestions to strengthen vocabulary, grammar and pronunciation.

Readings are authentic Canadian news articles. Each one is supported by vocabulary, comprehension and discussion activities.

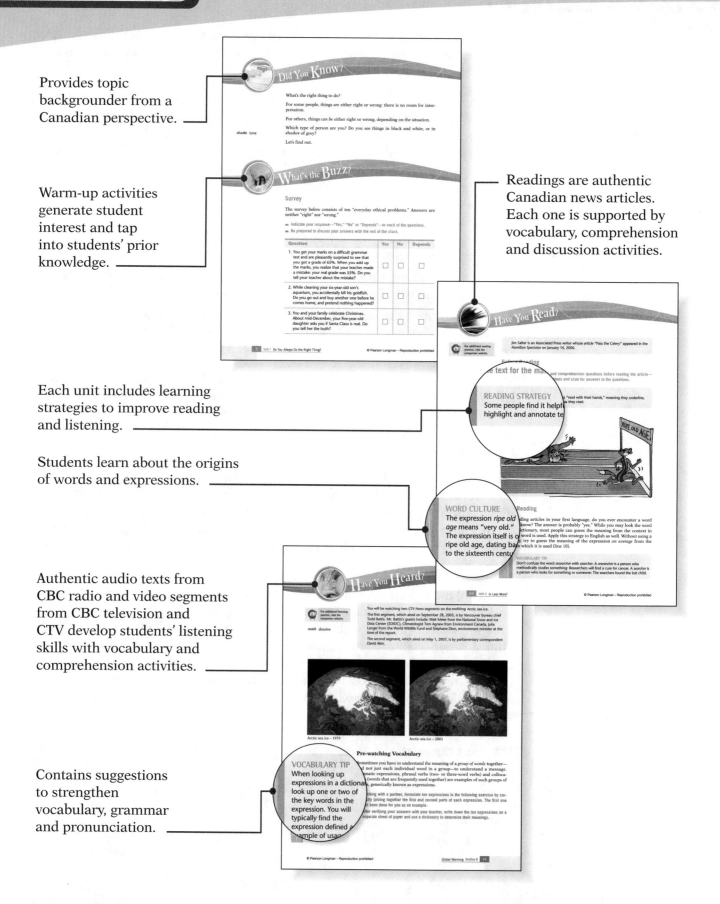

Students choose topics to develop in freeform or essay assignments.

Provides hints to improve writing and speaking skills.

A companion website provides additional reading, listening, writing and speaking practice.

Interactive activities facilitate the acquisition of new vocabulary.

Each unit ends with an activity that encourages cooperative learning.

- Supplementary articles provide students with further reading practice.

- Appendix A provides students with instructions and a model persuasive essay. Appendix B outlines the essentials of a presentation and gives detailed instructions on a debate.

Students can choose to discuss issues in a small group, give a presentation or participate in a debate.

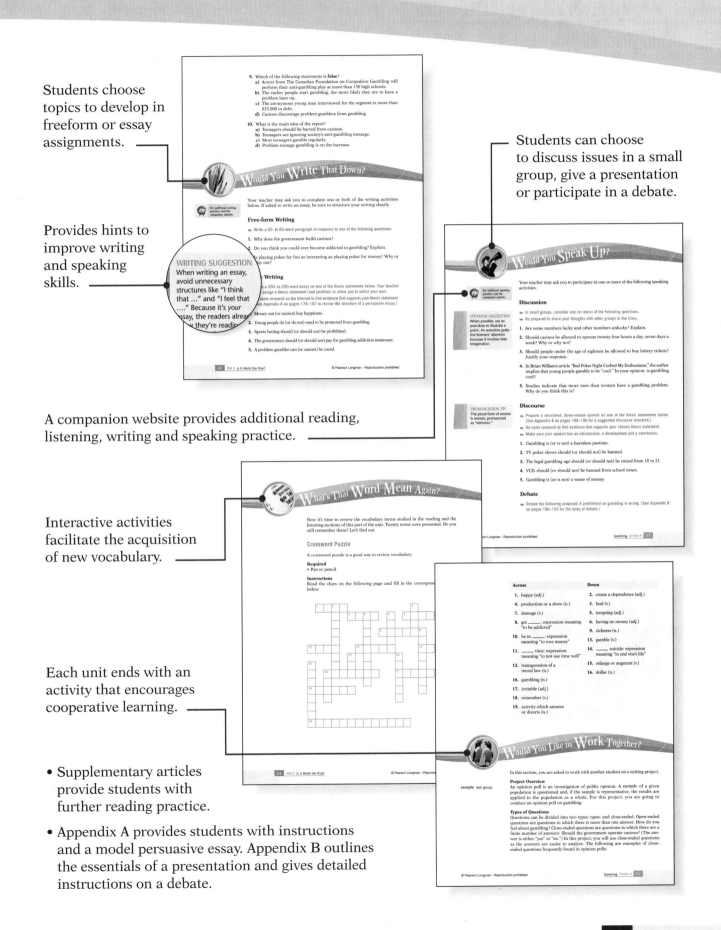

SCOPE AND SEQUENCE

Unit	Section	Reading	Listening/Watching
1. Do You *Always* Do the Right Thing?	Personal ethics	• Assess writing tone • Identify main and secondary ideas • Recognize phrasal verbs • Skim and scan for specific information	• Identify main and secondary ideas • Recognize vocabulary terms
2. Is It Beyond Our Control?	A. Gun Control B. Global Warming	• Examine divergent viewpoints • Identify main and secondary ideas	• Identify main and secondary ideas • Recognize transition terms
3. Is It Worth the Risk?	A. Gambling (VLTs) B. Cosmetic Surgery	• Examine divergent viewpoints • Identify main and secondary ideas • Assess reading context	• Identify main and secondary ideas • Appraise nonverbal communication (A) / apply techniques of concentration (B)
4. Is Less More?	A. Voluntary Simplicity B. Caloric Restriction	• Examine divergent viewpoints • Identify main and secondary ideas • Practise active reading	• Identify main and secondary ideas • Recognize optimal listening conditions
5. Are We Prisoners of Our Cells?	A. Restricting Juvenile Cellphone Usage B. Eugenics	• Examine divergent viewpoints • Identify main and secondary ideas • Organize information	• Identify main and secondary ideas • Organize information
6. Are We Too Protected?	A. Public Security B. Vaccination	• Examine divergent viewpoints • Identify main and secondary ideas • Organize information	• Identify main and secondary ideas • Apply existing knowledge

Writing	Speaking	Vocabulary	Critical Thinking
• Express opinions • Write a short paragraph • Write an individual or a group essay • Organize an essay • Research supporting points on the Internet • Apply correct referencing techniques	• Analyze ethical issues in small groups • Evaluate personal ethics • Formulate opinions • Justify positions • Identify anomalies • Relate a personal story	• Infer and memorize meanings • Apply terms in context • Know etymology of common idioms	• Create and revise a short story
• Express opinions • Write a short paragraph • Write and organize an essay • Employ sequencers • Research supporting points on the Internet • Apply correct referencing techniques	• Plan and complete a presentation • Practise using transition terms • Participate in a debate and demonstrate effective debating techniques • Discuss issues in small groups	• Formulate expressions and match expressions with meanings • Demonstrate understanding of terms • Know etymology of common idioms	• Construct and interpret a collage
• Express opinions • Write a short paragraph • Write and organize an essay • Write concisely • Research supporting points on the Internet • Apply correct referencing techniques	• Discuss issues in small groups • Illustrate opinions with anecdotes • Plan and complete a presentation • Participate in a debate and demonstrate effective debating techniques	• Match terms with definitions • Demonstrate understanding of terms • Know etymology of common idioms	• Conduct an opinion poll and analyze results
• Express opinions • Write a short paragraph • Write and organize an essay • Write legibly • Research supporting points on the Internet • Apply correct referencing techniques	• Discuss issues in small groups • Assess content significance • Plan and complete a presentation • Participate in a debate and demonstrate effective debating techniques • Express agreement and disagreement	• Determine meaning from context • Match terms with definitions • Recall and apply terms in context • Know etymology of common idioms	• Conduct an interview and synthesize responses
• Express opinions • Write a short paragraph • Write and organize an essay • Practise brainstorming techniques • Research supporting points on the Internet • Apply correct referencing techniques	• Discuss issues in small groups • Practise public speaking techniques • Plan and complete a presentation • Participate in a debate and demonstrate effective debating techniques	• Match terms with definitions • Demonstrate understanding of terms • Know etymology of common idioms	• Write and assess an op-ed piece
• Express opinions • Write a short paragraph • Write and organize an essay • Rate arguments • Research supporting points on the Internet • Apply correct referencing techniques	• Discuss issues in small groups • Defend a position • Plan and complete a presentation • Participate in a debate and demonstrate effective debating techniques	• Match terms with definitions • Recognize and apply terms • Know etymology of common idioms	• Write questions to summarize an article • Recognize verb tenses

TABLE OF CONTENTS

Unit 1: Do You *Always* Do the Right Thing? 1

Did You Know? 2
What's the Buzz? 2
Have You Read? 4
    "Stand Up and Do the Right Thing" by Brent Davis Reid 5
Have You Heard? 9
    "In People We Trust" by Terry Mosher
Would You Write That Down? 12
Would You Speak Up? 13
What's That Word Mean Again? (Crossword Puzzle) 16
Would You Like to Work Together? 17

Unit 2: Is It Beyond Our Control? 19

Section A: Gun Control 20
Did You Know? 20
What's the Buzz? 21
Have You Read? 22
    "Strengthen Gun Laws" from *The Barrie Examiner* 23
Have You Heard? 26
    "Anastasia's Law" and "Gun Registry in Rural Canada"
    from *CTV News* (Watching)
Would You Write That Down? 29
Would You Speak Up? 30
What's That Word Mean Again? (Word Search) 31
Would You Like to Work Together? 32

Section B: Global Warming 34
Did You Know? 34
What's the Buzz? 35
Have You Read? 36
    "Myths from Skeptics Slowing Us Down" by David Suzuki 37
Have You Heard? 41
    "Melting Arctic Sea Ice" from *CTV News* (Watching)
Would You Write That Down? 44
Would You Speak Up? 45
What's That Word Mean Again? (Word Search) 46
Would You Like to Work Together? 47

Unit 3: Is It Worth the Risk? 49

Section A: Gambling 50
Did You Know? 50
What's the Buzz? 51
Have You Read? 52
    "Bad Poker Night Curbed My Enthusiasm" by Brian Williams 53
Have You Heard? 57
    "Gambling and Suicide" and "Teen Gambling Addiction"
    from *CTV News* (Watching)
Would You Write That Down? 60
Would You Speak Up? 61
What's That Word Mean Again? (Crossword Puzzle) 62
Would You Like to Work Together? 63

Section B: Cosmetic Surgery 66
Did You Know? 66
What's the Buzz? 67
Have You Read? 68
   "Waiting a Lifetime for Plastic Surgery" by Ashley Bursey 69
Have You Heard? 72
   "Fountain of Youth" from *World Report*
Would You Write That Down? 75
Would You Speak Up? 76
What's That Word Mean Again? (Crossword Puzzle) 77
Would You Like to Work Together? 79

Unit 4: Is Less More? 81
Section A: Voluntary Simplicity 82
Did You Know? 82
What's the Buzz? 83
Have You Read? 84
   "Living Your Life without Worry" by Susan Semanak 85
Have Your Heard? 89
   "Interview with Issa" from *Radio Noon*
Would You Write That Down? 91
Would You Speak Up? 92
What's That Word Mean Again? (Hangman) 93
Would You Like to Work Together? 94

Section B: Caloric Restriction 95
Did You Know? 95
What's the Buzz? 97
Have You Read? 98
   "Pass the Celery: I'm Seventy but My Heart's Only Fifty-five" by Jim Salter . . . 99
Have You Heard? 103
   "Caloric Restriction Study" from *CTV News* (Watching)
Would You Write That Down? 106
Would You Speak Up? 106
What's That Word Mean Again? (Hangman) 107
Would You Like to Work Together? 108

Unit 5: Are We Prisoners of Our Cells? 110
Section A: Restricting Juvenile Cellphone Usage 111
Did You Know? 111
What's the Buzz? 112
Have You Read? 114
   "Do Phones Have a Role in School?" by Siobhan Bradley 115
Have You Heard? 118
   "Teen Drivers Using Cellphones" from *CTV News* (Watching)
Would You Write That Down? 121
Would You Speak Up? 122
What's That Word Mean Again? (Flash Cards) 123
Would You Like to Work Together? 124

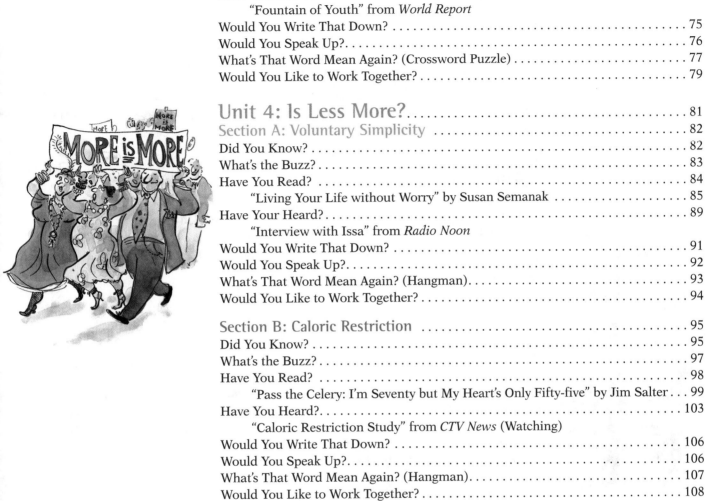

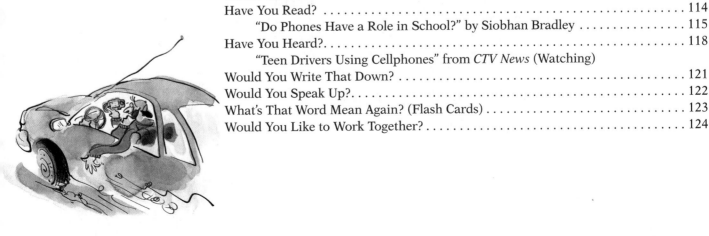

Section B: Eugenics 126
Did You Know? 126
What's the Buzz? 127
Have You Read? 129
    "'Culture of Perfection' Destroying Us" by Helen Henderson 130
Have You Heard? 133
    "Female Feticide" from *Our World* (Watching)
Would You Write That Down? 136
Would You Speak Up? 137
What's That Word Mean Again? (Flash Cards) 138
Would You Like to Work Together? 139

Unit 6: Are We Too Protected? 141

Section A: Public Security 142
Did You Know? 142
What's the Buzz? 143
Have You Read? 144
    "Exploding Pants Might Give Terrorists Ideas" by Les MacPherson 146
Have You Heard? 149
    "The List" from *The National* (Watching)
Would You Write That Down? 152
Would You Speak Up? 153
What's That Word Mean Again? 154
Would You Like to Work Together? 155

Section B: Vaccination 157
Did You Know? 157
What's the Buzz? 158
Have You Read? 159
    "Twelve Hours Later I Couldn't Raise My Legs—Polio Nightmare Lingers"
    by Gifford Jones 161
Have You Heard? 165
    "HPV Vaccination for Young Women" and
    "Vaccinating Young Children against Influenza"
    from *CTV News* (Watching) 165
Would You Write That Down? 168
Would You Speak Up? 169
What's That Word Mean Again? 170
Would You Like to Work Together? 172

Additional Reading
"If I Did Wrong, the Other Person Was at Fault, Okay?" by Lisa Fitterman 173
"Youth Gambling a Growing Concern" by Paul Barton 174
"Eating Fewer Calories Could Lead to Longer Life" by Lindsey Tanner 175
"On the Road" by Andrea Macko 176
"I'm Sick as a Dog—Literally" by Don Braid 177

Appendix A: The Persuasive Essay 178

Appendix B: Discourse and Debate 188

Do You *Always* Do the Right Thing?

Which of the following statements best describes you?

a) I **always** do the right thing.
b) I **usually** do the right thing.
c) I **often** do the right thing.
d) I **sometimes** do the right thing.
e) I **rarely** do the right thing.
f) I **never** do the right thing.

always	100%
usually	
often	
sometimes	
rarely	
never	0%

If you're like most people, your answer is neither a nor f as most people are neither saints nor sinners.

In this unit, you will be placed in a variety of situations in which you will have to decide whether to do the right thing (or not!). In later units, you will explore a variety of ethical issues drawn from the social and natural sciences.

Did You Know?

What's the right thing to do?

For some people, things *are* either right or wrong: there is no room for interpretation.

For others, things *can be* either right or wrong, depending on the situation.

Which type of person are you? Do you see things in black and white, or in **shades** of grey?

Let's find out.

shade tone

What's the Buzz?

Survey

The survey below consists of ten "everyday ethical problems." Answers are neither "right" nor "wrong."

- Indicate your response—"Yes," "No" or "Depends"—to each of the questions.
- Be prepared to discuss your answers with the rest of the class.

Question	Yes	No	Depends
1. You get your marks on a difficult grammar test and are pleasantly surprised to see that you got a grade of 65%. When you add up the marks, you realize that your teacher made a mistake: your real grade was 55%. Do you tell your teacher about the mistake?	☑	☐	☐
2. While cleaning your six-year-old son's aquarium, you accidentally kill his goldfish. Do you go out and buy another one before he comes home, and pretend nothing happened?	☐	☐	☑
3. You and your family celebrate Christmas. About mid-December, your five-year-old daughter asks you if Santa Claus is real. Do you tell her the truth?	☑	☐	☐

Question	Yes	No	Depends
4. Many people are waiting in line for the bus on a cold winter morning. Your coat is not very warm. You see an opening in the line. Do you cut in?	☐	☐	☐
5. You and your best friend go to the casino. You win $800; your friend loses $400. Do you compensate your friend's loss?	☐	☐	☐
6. It's **teeming**. You go to the dry cleaner to pick up your cleaning. The one parking spot available requires a disabled parking permit. You are not disabled and won't be there for more than a minute or two. Do you park your car in the disabled parking spot?	☐	☐	☐
7. A **panhandler** asks you for some change. You have a couple of **loonies** in your pocket. Do you give him one?	☐	☐	☐
8. Your biology teacher gives the same course to five different groups of students. She always gives the same test to each of her groups. You have already done the test. Your friend, who is in another group, hasn't. Your friend asks you what's on the test. Do you tell your friend what the questions are?	☐	☐	☐
9. You find a bus pass at the beginning of the month. A name and phone number are written on the back. You haven't bought your pass yet. Do you call the owner and return the pass?	☐	☐	☐
10. You learn that a local company is hiring one student for the summer. You and your best friend both need a job. Do you keep quiet about the job?	☐	☐	☐

teem rain very hard

panhandler person who asks strangers for money

loonie one-dollar Canadian coin

So, which type of person are you? Were all your answers either "yes" or "no" or did you sometimes indicate "depends"? In your opinion, did you always do the right thing?

VOCABULARY TIP
Say versus *tell*. The verb *say* means "to express": Her daughter says the funniest things. The verb *tell* means "to inform": Her son tells her everything. *Tell* is usually followed by an object.

Have You Read?

Brent Davis Reid is a college teacher and writer living in Quebec. His article "Stand Up and Do the Right Thing!" was inspired by his daily commute to work and is semi-autobiographical! His article was written for publication in this textbook.

READING STRATEGY
When reading an article, it is important to consider the tone. Is the tone serious or humorous? The article you're about to read is humorous. The humour comes from the author's use of exaggeration.

GRAMMAR TIP
The author uses many *phrasal verbs* in his article. Phrasal verbs consist of a verb and a preposition or adverb that changes the meaning: *get* means "to obtain" while *get on* means "to embark."

Before Reading

- Before reading the entire article, skim for the main ideas and scan for specific information.

How do you "skim and scan"? First, examine the ten words in **bold** print and their definitions in the margin. Then look over the reading comprehension questions at the end of the article. Finally, scan the text, <u>underlining</u> the answers to the questions. This is one way to "skim and scan."

While Reading

As you read, pay particular attention to how the words in **bold** are used.

- Try to read the whole article once without using a dictionary. Circle any words with which you're unfamiliar and try to understand what each word means from the context.
- Reread the article, using a dictionary to look up any words you couldn't understand.

STAND UP AND DO THE RIGHT THING!

BY BRENT DAVIS REID

It never fails.

No sooner do I park my tender tush in one of the highly sought-after seats of the Number 24 bus when an **elderly** passenger gets on and, as all the other seats are taken, stands directly next to "yours truly."

5 Typically said senior has five bags of **groceries**, a chronic cough and bears a striking resemblance to Mother Teresa of Calcutta.[1]

I feel my first pang of **guilt**.

I take out my newspaper—a *must* for travellers defending tired tootsies— and pretend to be absorbed in the daily crossword puzzle. Unfortunately 10 I have nothing with which to write, so my act falls flat. I **stare** at the empty grid, which strangely reminds me of a spider's web.

A childhood poem comes to mind:

Oh what a tangled web we weave when first we practise to deceive …[2]

I feel my second pang of guilt.

15 My companion coughs, the noise **barely** audible.

I maintain my stoic stance.

She coughs again, rather loudly this time.

I take out my iPod, hoping against hope to drown out the **racket**.

I sit back and wait for the music to transport me to a place far removed 20 from my present **predicament**. I wait, however, in vain. Ironically, the lyrics anchor me to my seat:

… Do the right thing baby do the right thing
Go with your heart and do the right thing …[3]

What's that I feel? Oh, yes. My third pang of guilt.

25 I am now fully **trapped** in our inverted staring contest: the moment I meet her gaze, I will lose.

I begin my mantra: I won't look. I won't look. I won't look.

Eventually, I look.

She says nothing. She doesn't need to.

30 I look away and **shift** slightly in my seat: I am not prepared to capitulate just yet.

The rationalizations begin.

elderly old

groceries food

guilt culpability

stare look intently

barely hardly

racket noise

predicament dilemma

trapped caught

shift move

I am tired. My feet are killing me. I am dying. (Okay, that last one isn't true: I'm as healthy as a horse. But *technically* we're all dying, right? No,
35 there is no straw at which I will not grasp!)

My justifications exhausted, I remove my earphones, put down my magazine and with a voice loud enough to be heard by everyone aboard I ask the long-anticipated question: "Excuse me, ma'am, would you like to sit down?"

40 With a solitary nod the deal is done.

trade exchange

I rise to my feet, we **trade** places and I imagine a day in the not-too-distant future when someone much younger than I will stand up for me and do the right thing.

427 words

1. Roman Catholic nun who devoted her life to the poor and sick of Calcutta
2. Sir Walter Scott. *Marmion, Canto vi. Stanza 17.*
3. George Strait. "Do the right thing" *Blue Clear Sky*

Reading Comprehension

▬ Respond to each of the questions.

1. A *euphemism* is an indirect term used to refer to something "indelicate." On line 2, the euphemism *tender tush* is used. To what does the euphemism refer?

   _____

   _____

2. The author claims that whenever he gets a seat on his bus, an older person always stands right beside him.   TRUE ☐   FALSE ☐

3. Why does the author begin to feel guilty?

   _____

   _____

4. Why is the author unable to do the crossword puzzle?

   _____

   _____

5. Why does the old woman cough more loudly the second time?

   _____

   _____

6. Why does the author feel even guiltier when listening to music?

   _____

   _____

7. Why does the author try not to look at the old woman?

_____

_____

8. What two **serious** reasons does the author give for not getting up?

a) _____

b) _____

9. Two expressions are used in the first paragraph on page 6. In your own words, what do these expressions mean?

a) to be healthy as a horse (line 34): _____

b) to grasp at straws (line 35): _____

10. What is the main idea of the article? Circle the letter of the correct answer.
a) Don't take public transportation.
b) Don't make eye contact while taking public transportation.
c) Sometimes, it costs you something to do the right thing.
d) People should feel guilty about not doing the right thing.

Reading Discussion

▬ In small groups, discuss your answers to the questions below. Arrive at a group consensus.

▬ On a separate sheet of paper, record your answers using the simple present tense.

▬ Be prepared to share your group's ideas with the rest of the class.

1. In the article, the author faces an ethical dilemma: stay comfortably seated while an elderly woman stands or make himself uncomfortable by giving up his seat. In your own words, explain why the author's dilemma is an ethical one.

2. Provide three examples of situations in which people choose personal comfort over doing the right thing.

3. What's easier—doing the right thing or the wrong thing? Explain.

Word Work

In the previous section, ten terms were defined for you:

Adjectives	Adverb	Nouns	Verbs
1. elderly 2. trapped	3. barely	4. groceries 5. guilt 6. predicament 7. racket	8. shift 9. stare 10. trade

GRAMMAR TIP
The simple present tense is used to express general or repeated actions and facts. Be sure to pronounce the final _s_ sound when using the third person singular (_he, she_ or _it_): He ~~stand~~ stands up.

© Pearson Longman – Reproduction prohibited

Do You _Always_ Do the Right Thing? Unit 1 7

■ Rewrite each of the sentences below, replacing the word or words in italics with one of the terms from the Word Work list (p. 7). The first one has been done for you as an example.

■ If you're replacing a verb, be sure to conjugate correctly.

1. He helps his *old* grandmother with the housework.
   He helps his elderly grandmother with the housework.
   _____

2. Could you *move* your bags please? I would like to sit down.
   _____
   _____

3. If he loses his job, he will be in quite a *dilemma*.
   _____
   _____

4. It's impolite to *look intently* at others.
   _____
   _____

5. Please ask the children to stop making all that *noise*!
   _____
   _____

6. She feels a lot of *culpability* about the divorce.
   _____
   _____

7. Someone's *caught* in the elevator. Could you call a technician?
   _____
   _____

8. Speak up! I can *hardly* hear you.
   _____
   _____

9. They go to the supermarket once a week to get *food*.
   _____
   _____

10. Would you like to *exchange* places with me?
    _____
    _____

Have You Heard?

For additional listening practice, visit the companion website.

Terry Mosher, who draws under the pen name Aislin, is an editorial cartoonist whose work has appeared in the *Montreal Gazette* for more than thirty years. On May 29, 2007, the Canadian Broadcasting Corporation's *This I Believe* series broadcast Mr. Mosher's personal reflections about a day in his life. Mr. Mosher entitled his piece "In People We Trust."

Pre-listening Vocabulary

Below you will find a series of ten quotes taken from the radio broadcast. Each quotation has a word (or words) in **bold**.

- Working alone or with a partner, try to infer the meaning of these words from the context.
- Then verify your inferences by looking them up in a dictionary.
- Use the chart at the end of this section to record your answers. The first one has been done for you as an example.

1. "Early this morning I had gum **surgery**, an arduous process that involved a lot of cutting, drilling and probing."

2. "A **segment** of my jawbone that had deteriorated over the years needed some shoring up …"

3. "When it was all over, the nurse … sent me on my way with a prescription for a **painkiller**."

4. "Leaving a nearby pharmacy, I **hailed** a taxi."

5. "My still partially frozen face kept **chit-chat** with colleagues to a minimum …"

6. "… but I did sit in on a 10 a.m. news meeting with *Gazette* editors to make sure **I was up to speed on the day's events**."

7. "My wife Mary … had **thought ahead** and brought me a nice bland lunch of yogurt and something or other …"

8. "The cartoon finished, I showed it as usual to my editors to get their O.K. and perhaps the odd **guffaw** …"

9. "Despite working in journalism, considered a **skeptical** business at best, I trust in the expertise of my editors and the composing room wizards …"

10. I even extend trust to the anonymous manufacturers of my pens, paper and computer! I realize that each and every day, I **take most of this for granted**.

Words	Inferred Meanings	Dictionary Definitions
1. surgery (noun)	*procedure*	*operation*
2. segment (noun)		
3. painkiller (noun)		
4. to hail (verb)		
5. chit-chat (noun)		
6. to be up to speed on something (expression)		

Words	Inferred Meanings	Dictionary Definitions
7. to think ahead (phrasal verb)		
8. guffaw (noun)		
9. skeptical (adjective)		
10. to take something for granted (expression)		

LISTENING STRATEGY
When listening for information, "skim and scan" as you do when reading for information. The first time, listen for the main idea. The second time, listen for the details.

While Listening

You will hear the segment twice.

■ Take notes as you listen and then respond to the comprehension questions.

Listening Comprehension

■ Referring to your notes, respond to each of the questions below.

1. To what is Terry Mosher's jawbone surgery compared?

_____

_____

2. During his surgery, Mr. Mosher was extremely agitated.   TRUE ☐ FALSE ☐

3. In addition to a prescription for a painkiller, what else did the nurse give Mr. Mosher?

_____

_____

4. What does Mr. Mosher do while he's driven to work in a taxi?

_____

_____

5. Mr. Mosher has trouble sketching his cartoon for the next day.   TRUE ☐ FALSE ☐

6. What does Mr. Mosher's wife do for a living?

_____

_____

7. What does Mary have for lunch that day?

_____

_____

© Pearson Longman – Reproduction prohibited

Do You *Always* Do the Right Thing? Unit 1   11

8. Once Terry's editors "okay" his cartoon, how is it sent to the composing room?

_____

_____

9. Who does Terry say he had to trust during his day?
a) the periodontist and his nurse
b) the pharmacist
c) the cab driver
d) his wife
e) his colleagues
f) the manufacturers of office supplies and equipment
g) all of the above

10. What is the main idea of the piece?
a) People can be trusted to do the right thing.
b) His colleagues are competent.
c) His wife is kind.
d) Montreal taxi drivers are good at their jobs.

Would You Write That Down?

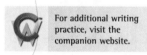

For additional writing practice, visit the companion website.

There are two types of writing assignments in this textbook: free-form and essay. In free-form writing, you are not obliged to follow a specific structure. In essay writing, you are obliged to follow a specific structure. An essay must have an introduction, a development and a conclusion.

There are many kinds of essays: descriptive, narrative and persuasive are three examples. Given the subject matter of *Parallels: Exploring the Issues*, your teacher will probably ask you to write a persuasive essay. You can find a detailed explanation and example of how to write a persuasive essay in Appendix A (pp. 178–187).

Free-form Writing

■ Write a 50- to 65-word paragraph in response to one of the following questions:

1. Why do many people distrust politicians?

2. Who do you trust? Why do you trust them?

3. Do you *always* do the right thing? Why or why not?

Essay Writing

- Write a 200- to 250-word essay on one of the thesis statements below. Your teacher may assign a thesis statement (and position) or allow you to select your own.
- Do some research on the Internet to find evidence that supports your thesis statement. (See Appendix A on pages 178–187 to review the structure of a persuasive essay.)

1. Young people should (or should not) give up their seats to elderly people on a bus.

2. Panhandling should (or should not) be permitted.

3. Lying is (or is not) sometimes right.

4. Exaggeration is (or is not) the same thing as lying.

5. Stealing is (or is not) always wrong.

WRITING SUGGESTION
When researching on the Internet, type key words into search engines such as google.ca or yahoo.ca.

Your teacher may ask you to work with a partner so that you can help each other learn the essay structure. If your teacher asks you to write a four-paragraph essay, divide up the work as follows:

- Both members write the first and fourth paragraphs together (the introduction and the conclusion);
- Each member writes one of the two body paragraphs individually; and
- Both members revise the completed essay together.

Would You Speak Up?

For additional speaking practice, visit the companion website.

As this is your first unit, you probably don't know the other students very well. To help you get to know one another better, your teacher may ask you to participate in one or more of the following small-group speaking activities.

Activity 1: Did They Do the Right Thing?

On page 14 you will find three scenarios. Each scenario deals with an ethical dilemma.

- In teams of three or four, read each of the scenarios and respond to the questions. For each scenario, your group must arrive at a consensus.
- Be prepared to discuss your answers with other groups in the class.

SPEAKING SUGGESTION
When speaking in public, always speak to the person farthest from you. In this way, you will speak loudly enough for everybody to hear!

WORD CULTURE
A *white lie* is a lie told to be polite or to avoid hurting someone's feelings. The expression dates back to the mid-1700s. In Scenario A, Karen told Steve a white lie.

© Pearson Longman – Reproduction prohibited

Do You *Always* Do the Right Thing? Unit 1   13

Scenario A: A White Lie

prom student dance held at the end of the year

show up arrive

Steve and Karen have been dating for a couple of months when Steve asks Karen to the **prom.** Karen is very excited and spends a lot of time and money on clothes and makeup. When the "big day" finally comes, Steve **shows up** wearing a baby blue tuxedo and running shoes. Karen is horrified! Steve tells Karen she looks great; to protect his feelings, Karen tells Steve he looks fantastic. Did Karen do the right thing? Explain.

Scenario B: A Lie of Omission

despite regardless of

strict severe

Despite the way Steve dressed for the prom, he and Karen get married. (No, Steve did not wear a baby blue tuxedo and running shoes to the wedding!) Both Steve and Karen are **strict** vegetarians; however, one day Steve *falls off the wagon* and eats a chicken Caesar salad for lunch. While Steve and Karen are having supper later that day, Karen asks him what he had for lunch. Steve says, "Oh, I had a salad." Did Steve do the right thing? Explain.

> **WORD CULTURE**
> The expression *to be on the wagon* typically refers to someone who has decided to stop drinking alcohol (but can refer to any state of abstinence). When one falls off the wagon, one starts to drink again. The expression dates back to a time in the American past when roads were made of dirt and needed to be sprayed with water by water wagons to keep down the dust. Men who had sworn off alcohol said they would rather climb on the water wagon to drink water than drink alcohol ever again.

barefaced lie manifest lie

affair sexual relationship

Scenario C: A Barefaced Lie

A couple of years down the road, Steve gets the *seven year itch*. Despite his best intentions to remain faithful, he has a brief **affair** with a married colleague. Karen asks Steve if he has ever cheated on her. In order not to lose Karen, Steve tells her that he has always been faithful. Did Steve do the right thing? Explain.

> **WORD CULTURE**
> The expression *the seven year itch* refers to a desire to change one's sexual partner after seven years of marriage. The expression was popularized in the mid-1950s by *The Seven Year Itch*, a movie starring Marilyn Monroe.

Scenarios A, B and C: Wrap-Up

Look at your answers to the above scenarios. Does your group think that some lies are right and some lies are wrong? If so, explain.

Activity 2: Which Statement Is True?

Can others tell when you're lying? Do you know when they're lying? That's what we're about to find out.

- On a separate sheet of paper, write down two statements about yourself, one true and one untrue. Your statements should be written in the simple present tense. For example:
  1) I write books. (This statement is true.)
  2) I play hockey every weekend. (This statement is untrue.)
  Choose statements you think are interesting.

- Find a partner and read your two statements aloud.

- Your partner will question you about your statements to determine which statement is true. For example:
  1) What kind of books do you write?
  2) When do you write?
  3) Where do you play hockey?
  4) What position do you play?

  Note: Your partner is not allowed to simply ask you which statement is true.
- When your partner no longer has any questions, he or she must tell you which statement he or she thinks is true. Tell your partner whether he or she is right.
- Repeat the activity: this time your partner reads his or her statements and you do the questioning.

VOCABULARY TIP
See Appendix A in *Parallels: Exploring the Issues English Grammar* to review common information question words.

Activity 3: What's Wrong with This Picture?

The picture below was inspired by the reading passage of this unit.

- In teams of three or four, identify ten things wrong with the picture.
- Do not use a dictionary.
- Your teacher will ask your group how many mistakes you were able to find and then ask you to explain them. The group that finds the most mistakes wins!

© Pearson Longman – Reproduction prohibited

Do You *Always* Do the Right Thing? Unit 1   15

Now it's time to review the vocabulary terms studied in the reading and the listening sections of this unit. Twenty terms were presented. Do you still remember them?

Crossword Puzzle

A crossword puzzle is a fun way to review vocabulary.

Required
• Pen or pencil

Instructions
Read the clues on the following page and fill in the corresponding blanks below.

Across	Down
3. noise	**1.** analgesic
6. dilemma	**2.** move
7. conversation	**4.** plan ahead (expression): _____ ahead
8. culpability	**5.** food
9. operation	**9.** look intently
10. old	**11.** be sore
12. exchange	**14.** loud laugh
13. part	**16.** call over
15. not fully appreciate something (expression): take something for _____ .	**17.** be informed about something (expression): be up to _____ on something
17. cynical	
18. hardly	

Would You Like to Work Together?

In this section, you will work with another student on a writing project.

Project Overview

In this unit, you read "Stand Up and Do the Right Thing!", a short story about a passenger who struggles over giving up his seat on a bus (pp. 5–6). For this project, you and your partner are asked to write a 150- to 200-word short story entitled "A White Lie."

Writing a Short Story

A good short story is often based on real experience; for this reason, you are asked to base your short story on an experience that one of you has had.

Procedure

1. Review the meaning of the expression "a white lie." (See Word Culture box, page 13.)

2. Talk about white lies you have told.

3. Choose the white lie you find most interesting and write a short story *based on* this experience. (Remember: You are not writing about what happened; you are writing a short story inspired by a real experience.)

4. Use the first person singular (*I*) and the present tenses (simple and continuous); the story "Stand Up and Do the Right Thing" serves as a model.

5. As you write, embellish (invent or exaggerate) the details.

draft version

6. After you have finished your first **draft**, revise your work: check your spelling, verify your grammar (especially your verb conjugations) and use a thesaurus (a book of synonyms) and a dictionary to help you find the right words.

7. Write a second draft, incorporating the changes made while revising the first. Write legibly (or use a word processor) and double-space your work. Include a word count at the end of your story.

8. Submit your story to your teacher for evaluation.

UNIT 2 Is It Beyond Our Control?

Something beyond our control is something we cannot influence.

The weather, for example, is beyond our control: we have no choice but to accept whatever Mother Nature gives us.

Some people believe gun control and global warming are beyond society's control.

Others disagree.

What do you think? Let's explore the issues and find out.

SECTION A
Gun Control

Examines the issue of gun registration.

SECTION B
Global Warming

Examines whether people should take action to stop global warming.

Gun Control

Did You Know?

Canada has a long history of gun control dating back to the late 1800s. As early as 1892, Canadians needed permits to carry handguns outside their homes.

firearm gun

Since the passing of "The Firearms Act" in 1995, Canadians are legally required to have a licence to own a **firearm** and must register all firearms with the Canadian Gun Registry, a government-run registry of legally owned weapons.

city urban area
country rural area

Supporters of the gun registry typically live in the **city** where criminal acts are frequent, while opponents of the gun registry typically live in the **country** where criminal acts are comparatively infrequent.

The chart on page 21 summarizes two arguments *in support of* gun registration and two arguments *in opposition to* gun registration.

Gun registration is right because it	Gun registration is wrong because it
1. prevents crime.	1. does not prevent crime.
2. saves lives.	2. is expensive.

Do you support gun registration, or do you oppose it?

Answer this question now, and again after you have completed this unit.

Do you think your answer will stay the same? Only time will tell.

What's the Buzz?

How much do you know about guns and gun violence in Canada? Take the following quiz and find out.

■ **Choose the correct answers.**

1. In 2000, there were approximately _____ firearm owners in Canada.
   a) 750 000   **c)** 5 million
   b) 2.3 million   **d)** 10 million

wound injury

2. How many Canadians die every year from gunshot **wounds**?
   a) less than 100   **c)** 500 to 1000
   b) 100 to 500   **d)** more than 1000

3. Most gunshot deaths in Canada are:
   a) suicides   **b)** accidents   **c)** homicides

4. In 1998, more than half of the homicides committed in Canada involved guns.   TRUE ☐ FALSE ☐

5. In 1998, _____ of robberies involved guns.
   a) 8%   **b)** 18%   **c)** 80%

Discussion

■ Get into small groups.
■ Consider the questions at the top of page 22 and arrive at a consensus. Use a dictionary to look up any difficult terms.
■ Present your ideas to the rest of the class.

1. Are you surprised at the answers to any of the questions on page 21? If so, which one(s)?

2. In your opinion, is there more crime in the city or in the country? Explain.

3. Do you think it's a good idea to have a gun in your house for protection? Justify your response.

Have You Read?

For additional reading practice, visit the companion website.

An editorial piece is an article written by a member of the editorial staff of a newspaper. Typically, an editorial expresses the opinion of the editor(s) about a controversial issue of the day. The editorial you are about to read concerns gun control and refers to the shootings at two Montreal schools: Dawson College on September 13, 2006, and the École Polytechnique on December 6, 1989. The article appeared in *The Sault Star* on September 25, 2006, and was written by the editorial staff of the *Barrie Examiner*.

Before Reading

Remember to skim and scan before reading: *first* read the defined terms and comprehension questions, and *then* read the article.

While Reading

Transition words demonstrate relationships between ideas. Examples of transition words include *and, so, but,* etc.

■ As you read, circle any transition terms used by the author. Being aware of transition terms will help you better follow the author's train of thought.

NOT AGAIN!

STRENGTHEN GUN LAWS

BARRIE EXAMINER

inescapable inevitable

midday noon

wounded injured
swift immediate

weapon gun

deter discourage

background personal history

wear be dressed in

matter be important

twice two times

Canada's gun-control laws don't work. That's the **inescapable** conclusion from the shootings at a downtown Montreal college, where a heavily armed man opened fire on the campus at **midday**.

5 One person was killed, twenty others **wounded**—five critically—before police shot the gunman dead. Only **swift** response by police—on site within three minutes of the man opening fire—prevented even more carnage.

The gunman was armed to the teeth, by all accounts. There are reports he was carrying a 12-gauge shotgun, a 9-mm pistol and a semi-automatic rifle. Sources also say all of these **weapons** had been legally purchased 10 and registered, and under the man's own name.

To this point, much of the gun control debate in this country has focused on illegal weapons, such as handguns. The argument is that the long-gun registry does nothing to **deter** crime, that it only regulates hunters, collectors and farmers. And handguns are already severely restricted in 15 Canada, with a registry in force for more than sixty years. So, how is it that this Montreal college gunman had these weapons, let alone possessed them legally? What possible reasons could there be for the authorities allowing him to have these guns?

During the next days, weeks and months, the dead gunman's **background** 20 will be investigated by both the police and national media. There are already stories about his love of weapons and heavy metal music. He **was wearing** a long, black leather trenchcoat and leather boots, had multiple body piercings and spiked hair.

That will be enough information for many Canadians to judge him.

25 None of this would **matter**, however, if he hadn't been able to lay his hands on a semi-automatic rifle, a shotgun and a pistol.

Perhaps most importantly, Canadian police refer to the registry five thousand times a day.

None of this, however, is enough.

30 It's still far too easy for people to legally get their hands on weapons. And it's still far too easy for people to get their hands on illegal weapons.

What Canadians want to know, and what Canadians need to know, is how this Montreal gunman got his weapons and what can be done so that it doesn't happen again.

35 If this means changing the laws so it's more difficult to possess certain types of handguns or rifles in this country, then so be it.

Because **twice** in seventeen years is two times too many, and it needs to end.

409 words

Reading Comprehension

■ **Respond to each of the questions.**

1. What two-word expression in the first paragraph means "started shooting"?

   _____

2. Why were more people not killed or wounded?

   _____

3. What expression in paragraph 3 means "have many weapons"?

   _____

4. In paragraph 3, three types of weapons are listed. Name them.

   _____

5. The gunman's weapons were unregistered.   TRUE ☐ FALSE ☐

6. Handguns have always been restricted in Canada.   TRUE ☐ FALSE ☐

7. In your own words, describe the gunman.

   _____

   _____

8. What expression in lines 25–26 means "to get a hold of" or "to secure"?

   _____

9. Canadian police rarely consult the gun registry.   TRUE ☐ FALSE ☐

10. What is the main point of the editorial?
    a) Handguns should be banned.
    b) Gun-control laws should be reinforced.
    c) Shootings need to end.
    d) Gun violence cannot be stopped.

Reading Discussion

■ **In small groups, discuss your answers to each of the questions below. Arrive at a consensus.**

■ **Be prepared to share your group's ideas with the rest of the class.**

1. In your opinion, was the gunman's appearance menacing? Explain.

2. Should people living in urban areas be allowed to own guns? People living in rural areas? Justify your response.

3. How do you feel about hunting for food? For sport?

Word Work

In the previous section, ten new words were defined for you:

Adjectives	Adverb	Nouns	Verbs
1. inescapable 2. swift 3. wounded	4. twice	5. background 6. midday 7. ~~weapon~~	8. deter 9. matter 10. wear

■ Reread the definitions provided for these words. Then reread the sentences in which the words are used to ensure you understand how each word is used in context.

■ Fill in the blanks using the words above. Remember to conjugate the verbs as required. The first one has been done for you as an example.

1. Airport security is very tight. Anyone suspected of carrying a ___*weapon*___ is searched.

2. Death, like taxes, is _____!

3. Do you think that long prison sentences _____ crime?

4. He asked her to marry him _____; the second time around, she accepted his offer.

5. I never eat breakfast, so I'm usually very hungry by _____.

6. Sometimes, fashion models _____ the most ridiculous clothes!

7. The lifeguards' _____ response saved the swimmer's life.

8. Unfortunately, soldiers are often killed or _____ in war.

9. What _____ to you? Friends and family or fame and fortune?

10. When you apply for a job, the interviewers will ask you questions about your _____. They will want to know about your education, past employment and current pastimes.

For additional listening practice, visit the companion website.

bill proposed legislation

rampage series of violent acts

You will be watching two *CTV News* segments on gun control legislation.

In the first segment, which aired on June 15, 2007, Jed Kahane files a report on "Anastasia's Law,"[1] a **bill** named after Anastasia De Sousa who was killed by Kimveer Gill during a shooting **rampage** at Dawson College in September of 2006. Featured guests include Dawson shooting victim Hayder Khadim, the parents of Anastasia (Louise and Nelson De Sousa), gun-club owner Michel Giroux and Quebec premier Jean Charest.

In the second segment, which aired on June 17, 2004, *CTV News* reporter Joy Malbon visits Yorkton, Saskatchewan where she interviews local residents about gun registration. Featured guests include hunter Doug Hacking, farmer George Chornomud, minister Dave Taylor and gun-shop owner Terry Chornomud (TC).

Worlds apart?

Pre-watching Vocabulary

Sometimes you have to understand the meaning of a *group of words* together—and not just each individual word in a group—to understand a message. Idiomatic expressions, phrasal verbs (two- or three-word verbs) and collocations (words that are frequently used together) are examples of such groups of words, generically known as expressions.

▬ Working with a partner, formulate ten expressions in the following exercise by correctly joining together the first and second parts of each expression. The first one has been done for you as an example.

---

1. "Anastasia's Law" makes it illegal to have firearms near educational centres or to carry them on most public transit systems (CTV.ca News Staff, "De Sousas still want answers about day of shooting.")

- After verifying your answers with your teacher, write down the ten expressions on a separate sheet of paper and use a dictionary to determine their meanings.

Segment 1

First Part		Second Part
1. in the wake	_b_	a) concerns
2. keep	____	b) of something
3. raise	____	c) in person
4. show up	____	d) to now
5. up	____	e) records

Segment 2

First Part		Second Part
6. bear	____	f) up somebody about something
7. burning	____	g) arms
8. fire	____	h) issue
9. make	____	i) off
10. ward	____	j) or break

VOCABULARY TIP
When looking up expressions in a dictionary, look up one or two of the key words in the expression. You will typically find the expression defined and an example of usage given near the end of the entry. You will need a *good* dictionary for this type of exercise!

While Watching

You will watch the segment twice.

- The first time you watch, try to understand the speakers' main ideas.
- The second time you watch, listen for the details of what each speaker has to say, taking brief notes to help you remember the information.

LISTENING STRATEGY
Transition terms not only help you follow a writer's thoughts, but they help you follow a speaker's thoughts as well. Actively listen for the transition words used by the speakers.

Watching Comprehension

- Referring to your notes, respond to each of the questions below.

Segment 1
1. In which part of his body was Hayder Khadim shot?

_____

2. Circle the letter(s) of the correct answer(s). More than one response is possible. Gunman Kimveer Gill:
   a) was depressed.
   b) tried to hide his violent tendencies.
   c) owned his guns legally.

3. The proposed gun legislation calls for an increase in Internet surveillance, requires that applications for gun licences be made in person and that mental health professionals report dangerous patients. What two things must gun-club owners do?

a) _____

b) _____

4. Gun-club owner Michel Giroux believes that although the proposed gun legislation will unfortunately increase paperwork, the legislation will make the public safer. TRUE ☐ FALSE ☐

5. Which of the following statements best summarizes the main idea of the report?
a) Canadian gun-control legislation goes too far.
b) Canadian gun-control legislation does not go far enough.
c) Canadian provincial and federal governments agree on gun-control legislation.
d) Canadians and their governments disagree on gun-control legislation.

Segment 2
6. In Yorkton, Saskatchewan, the gun registry is still a charged issue. TRUE ☐ FALSE ☐

7. For farmer George Chornomud, a rifle is not a weapon; it is a tool which he uses to kill varmints (wild animals) such as coyotes, mink and racoons that prey on his chickens. TRUE ☐ FALSE ☐

8. Fill in the blanks.

Journalist: "It's kind of hard to find a _____

_____ around here. Even the church minister, Dave

Taylor, owns half a dozen guns or so."

Dave Taylor: "When you think of … it's a heritage … we really believe …

I really believe … if there's a right to _____

_____ …."

9. Gun-shop owner "TC" points to a loophole (or ambiguity) in the gun registry system. What is the loophole?

_____

10. Which of the following statements best summarizes the main idea of the report?
a) The gun registry is extremely unpopular with the residents of Yorkton, Saskatchewan.
b) The residents of Yorkton, Saskatchewan are divided on the gun registry issue.
c) The government should stop spending billions of dollars on the gun registry.
d) The government should abolish the gun registry and lower taxes.

Would You Write That Down?

There are two types of writing assignment below. Free-form writing has no specific structure; essay writing does. If your teacher asks you to write an essay, be sure to respect the structure requested.

Free-form Writing

▬ Write a 50- to 65-word paragraph in response to one of the following questions:

carry out execute

1. The Dawson College and École Polytechnique shootings were both **carried out** by men. Is this fact significant? Explain.

2. People who are opposed to gun control claim that, "… guns don't kill people. People kill people." What do they mean by this statement?

3. What is the most important thing society can do to prevent another school shooting? Justify your choice.

Essay Writing

▬ Write a 200- to 250-word essay on one of the thesis statements below. Your teacher may assign a thesis statement (and position) or allow you to select your own.

▬ Do some research on the Internet to find evidence that supports your thesis statement. (See Appendix A on pages 178–187 to review the structure of a persuasive essay.)

1. People should (or should not) be allowed to own guns.

2. Hunting should (or should not) be banned.

carry have something with you

3. Police officers should (or should not) **carry** guns.

4. Gun owners should (or should not) be obligated to take a course in gun safety.

5. Police officers should (or should not) use tasers.

VOCABULARY TIP
Should is a modal, a special verb used with other verbs to express a particular mood: Eliot should study. *Should* expresses advisability or desirability. Modals are invariable: Eliza ~~shoulds~~ should do her homework.

WRITING SUGGESTION
A sequencer is a special type of transition word. Examples include "first," "second," etc. When writing an essay, use sequencers to help the reader follow your ideas.

Would You Speak Up?

For additional speaking practice, visit the companion website.

Your teacher may ask you to participate in one or more of the following speaking activities.

Discussion

- In small groups, consider one (or more) of the following questions.
- Be prepared to share your thoughts with other groups in the class.

1. Why do people own guns? Give at least two reasons.

2. Is your generation more violent than your parents' generation? Justify your response.

safe secure

3. Do you feel **safe** at school? Why or why not?

4. Why do some people enjoy watching films with gun violence?

5. Does the issue of gun control concern you personally? Why or why not?

SPEAKING SUGGESTION
Use transition words (*and, so, but, first, second*, etc.) when you're speaking to help the listener follow along.

Discourse

- Prepare a structured, three-minute speech on one of the thesis statements below. (See Appendix B on pages 188–190 for a suggested speech structure.)
- Do some research to find evidence that supports your chosen thesis statement. Make sure your speech has an introduction, a development and a conclusion.

1. Children should (or should not) be allowed to hunt.

2. Video games with gun violence should (or should not) be banned.

3. The legal minimum age of gun ownership in Canada should (or should not) be raised from 18 to 21.

4. Metal detectors should (or should not) be installed in schools.

5. School security guards should (or should not) be armed.

Debate

- Debate the following proposal: Gun registration is wrong. (See Appendix B on pages 190–193 for the rules of debate.)

What's That Word Mean Again?

Twenty terms were presented in this part of Unit 2: ten from the reading section and ten from the watching section. Go back and review these words and then test your vocabulary by completing the activity below.

Word Search

In the activity below, you'll be looking for the vocabulary words from Section A of this unit. Do you think you can find the words? Let's find out.

Required
• Pen or pencil

Instructions
1. For 1–10, decide which words the definitions represent, and for 11–20, decide which words are missing.

2. Find these words in the grid. (Words can go forward and backward, horizontally, vertically and diagonally.)

3. When you're finished, the first 56 unused letters in the grid will spell out a famous quotation: to uncover the quotation, pick out the letters from left to right, moving from the top line down to the bottom line.

4. Rewrite these letters, in order, in the space provided below the grid.

Definitions

1. inevitable
2. noon
3. injured
4. immediate
5. gun
6. discourage
7. personal history
8. be dressed in
9. be important
10. two times

11. immediately after something (expression): in the _____ of something
12. keep track of information (expression): _____ _____
13. be troubling (expression): _____ _____
14. arrive in person (expression): _____ _____ in person
15. until this time (expression): _____ _____ _____
16. carry weapons (expression): _____ _____
17. important question (expression): _____ _____
18. get somebody going about something (expression): _____ _____ somebody about something
19. cause to succeed or to fail (expression): make or _____
20. protect against (expression): _____ off

E	R	A	I	S	E	C	O	N	C	E	R	N	S	T
L	E	H	D	N	U	O	R	G	K	C	A	B	E	H
B	T	U	M	A	N	S	M	R	A	R	A	E	B	K
A	T	R	A	F	I	R	E	U	P	U	C	Y	E	E
P	A	W	O	U	N	D	E	D	P	D	A	U	E	E
A	M	H	A	S	O	N	E	T	E	D	S	R	C	P
C	E	A	S	L	L	Y	O	T	D	S	E	I	F	R
S	F	E	C	H	T	N	E	I	I	I	W	D	V	E
E	E	W	E	S	O	R	M	G	A	T	P	R	O	C
N	N	A	N	W	W	W	N	D	W	T	H	A	A	O
I	W	A	K	E	R	I	U	T	E	I	S	W	L	R
A	U	G	H	A	N	A	F	P	A	T	E	R	G	D
R	X	V	L	R	E	C	E	T	P	L	M	F	B	S
T	R	P	U	N	V	R	M	W	O	H	L	P	F	R
F	D	B	L	X	X	Z	B	B	N	H	K	Q	M	Z

Famous quotation: ___ _____ ____ ___ ___ _____

_____ _____ ___ ____ __ _____.

Would You Like to Work Together?

In this section, you will work with another student on a speaking project.

Project Overview

A collage is a picture made by sticking photographs, magazine or newspaper cutouts, etc., onto a surface. Collages can be constructed to make a political point. An effective collage makes audiences think and feel deeply about a given subject—graphic content is chosen for its strong visual impact. You and your partner must construct a collage that reflects *what you think* and *how you feel* about gun control. When finished, you will present your collage to the class.

Procedure

1. Work with a partner who shares your thoughts and feelings about gun control.
   Note: Your teacher may choose to assign partners.

2. Discuss your thoughts and feelings about gun control.

3. List your thoughts and feelings in point form on a separate sheet of paper. Be sure to write your names at the top of the sheet.

4. Decide what your message is. (Ask yourselves what statement you would like your collage to make.)

5. Working individually, go through magazines, newspapers, etc., and cut out images that will help make your message.

6. Working together, go through the cutouts and select ten images that, when assembled, will best transmit your message.

7. On a large piece of light-coloured bristol board (56 cm x 71 cm), arrange your ten images. Note: Feel free to add graphic content (lines, arrows, etc.)—**but do not write down any words**! Let the pictures speak for themselves.

8. On the reverse side of your collage, write down ten key words that will help you present your collage—one word for each image. You may wish to use a dictionary.

9. Present your collage to your class. First describe the images, referring to key words as necessary. Second, ask members of your class to interpret your collage. (See if the message you intended to send was the one they actually received!) Finally, reveal your message to the class.

10. Graciously accept your audience's applause!

Assignment Submission
Submit your collage as well as your list of thoughts and feelings (see point 3 above) to your teacher for evaluation.

Global Warming

Did You Know?

thrive prosper

Life on earth **thrives** due to the greenhouse effect, a natural occurrence wherein heat radiating from the earth is trapped by greenhouse gases, such as carbon dioxide, methane and nitrous oxide. Without the greenhouse effect, the earth's temperature would be approximately 33 °C colder than it is—making life on this planet difficult, if not impossible.

Statistics on average global annual temperatures have been recorded since 1861 and analysis of these statistics demonstrates that the earth has been getting warmer, particularly within the last **decade**.

decade ten years

The causes of global warming remain a matter of public debate for some people.

On the one hand, there are global warming skeptics who argue that the earth's temperature has always varied. For them, the earth's current warming period is caused by nature.

On the other hand, there are global warming believers who maintain that the burning of fossil fuels has increased greenhouse gases, accentuating the greenhouse effect. For them, the earth's current warming period is caused by human activity.

WORD CULTURE
The expression *come what may* means "whatever happens." The expression originated in the 1500s and exists in many languages.

At the heart of the issue is the following question: should humans act to stop global warming? Or should we do nothing and simply accept come what may?

Actions to stop global warming are right because	Actions to stop global warming are wrong because
1. global warming is caused by human activity.	1. global warming is caused by nature.
2. global warming is environmentally destructive.	2. they are economically destructive.

What's the Buzz?

How much do you know about climate change? Take the following quiz and find out.

Choose the correct answers. In some questions, more than one answer is possible.

1. Joseph Fourier discovered the greenhouse effect in:
   a) 1800   **b)** 1824   **c)** 1901

2. Which of the following are examples of fossil fuels that, when burned, contribute to greenhouse gases by releasing carbon dioxide?
   a) coal   **b)** oil   **c)** natural gas

3. According to *CBC News* ("Carbon offset"), the average Canadian generates _____ tons of greenhouse gases a year, more than double the amount created by citizens in the United Kingdom or Sweden.
   a) 11   **b)** 22   **c)** 33

4. The United Nations Intergovernmental Panel on Climate Change (IPCC) predicts in a 2007 report that in addition to rising temperatures, some of the potential consequences of global warming include:
   a) higher sea levels   **c) droughts**
   b) heat waves   **d)** intense hurricanes

drought long period of no rain

5. The IPCC predicts that the average global temperature will increase between _____ and _____ degrees Celsius in the next 100 years.
   a) 1.8 and 4   **b)** 4 and 6   **c)** 6 and 8

Discussion

- Get into small groups.
- Consider the questions below and arrive at a consensus. Use a dictionary to look up any difficult terms.
- Present your ideas to the rest of the class.

1. Does climate change worry you? Explain.

2. Do any of your daily actions contribute to greenhouse gases? If so, which ones?

3. What do you do (or not do) to preserve the environment?

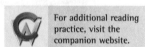

For additional reading practice, visit the companion website.

David Suzuki is a well-known Canadian scientist, environmental activist and TV personality. He is host of the popular CBC science program *The Nature of Things* and is the author of more than 30 books. His article "Myths from Skeptics Slowing Us Down" appeared in the *Owen Sound Sun Times* on May 25, 2007. From the title, can you guess how Mr. Suzuki feels about people who doubt global warming is happening?

READING STRATEGY
When skimming for main ideas, pay careful attention to the title of an article. The title often reveals the author's opinion on a subject.

Before Reading

- Remember to skim and scan before reading: *first* read the defined terms and comprehension questions, and *then* read the article.

While Reading

Transition words demonstrate relationships between ideas. Examples of transition words include *and, or, however,* etc. As you read, circle any transition terms used by the author. Being aware of transition terms will help you better follow the author's train of thought.

> **GRAMMAR TIP**
> *Bad ... worse ... worst. Bad* is an adjective: Steve got a bad grade. *Worse* is a comparative adjective, used to compare two people or things: Steve's grade is worse than Charlie's. *Worst* is a superlative adjective, used to compare three or more people or things: Steve's grade is the worst in the class.

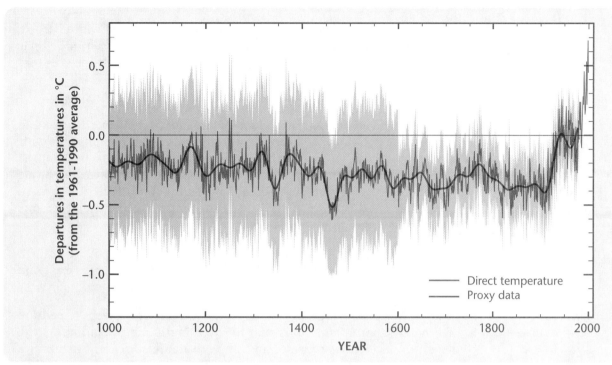

Variations of the Earth's Surface Temperature for the Past 1000 Years (Northern Hemisphere)

VOCABULARY TIP
The verb *occur* means "to take place." The verb *arrive* means "to get to a place."
The accident ~~arrived~~ occurred just before lunch; the police arrived quickly.

MYTHS FROM SKEPTICS SLOWING US DOWN

BY DAVID SUZUKI

in spite of even with

lack insufficiency

In spite of explosive news coverage about global warming over the past year, most people still have only a very rudimentary knowledge of this complex issue. Unfortunately, this **lack** of knowledge has led to persistent myths, which are slowing down real action that could prevent the worst
5 damage from occurring to our economy and to our environment.

worry be concerned
hectic busy
scary terrifying

Most of us are just too busy to get to the bottom of climate science. It's undeniably complicated and it's more than most people want to deal with in their daily lives. We all have to **worry** about our jobs, our families and just getting through **hectic** days. Global warming is **scary** and we hope
10 someone does something about it, or tells us what to do.

mislead dupe

For some, however, doubting the science of global warming has taken on an almost religious zeal. Those blessed with "knowledge" shake their heads sadly at people who are concerned about a warming planet and are trying to do something about it. They pontificate about how the public
15 has been **misled** by a few (usually European) academics who rely on "faulty" computer models, socialist biases or both.

Talking to these people is hard because they come armed with obscure-sounding references about things like the "medieval warm period," "solar flares" and "hockey-stick" graphs.[1] They seem so sure of themselves that
20 the media still routinely feature these so-called global warming skeptics in opinion articles, television interviews and especially on talk radio.

Media outlets love these guys (yes, they are mostly men and they tend to be the same, often paid, "experts" over and over again) because they stir things up. These guys specialize in arguing and confusing people, the
25 same way tobacco industry lobbyists did and still do. Having people argue on talk radio is that medium's bread and butter. And what better way to get people **riled up** than to have a self-proclaimed "expert" tell everyone that global warming is a myth?

riled up enraged

The problem is that some people believe it. Or, more often, it creates just
30 enough doubt for people—including politicians—to ignore the issue. And that's dangerous ....

reduce diminish

Many governments are still stalling on taking substantial steps to **reduce** the heat-trapping emissions that are causing global warming. As the scientific academies representing thirteen nations recently wrote in a
35 joint statement on climate protection: "The problem is not yet insoluble, but becomes more difficult with each passing day."

debunk refute

That's why it's so important to **debunk** these myths and move on. They're slowing us down at a time when delay makes the problem more and more costly, and more and more difficult to **fix**. If you want to help, ... arm
40 yourself with knowledge, then tell a friend or, even better, an elected leader and take down these myths once and for all.

fix repair

470 words

1. The term "hockey-stick" graph refers to a graph of temperature trends over the last 1000 years as constructed by Michael Mann et al. The trend line resembles hockey sticks. (*Wikipedia*. "Michael Mann." Retrieved: 10 July 2007. http://en.wikipedia.org/wiki/Michael_Mann_(scientist))

Reading Comprehension

▬ Respond to each of the questions.

1. Media do not pay enough attention to the issue of global warming. TRUE ☐ FALSE ☐

2. Why do most people know so little about global warming? (Hint: There are two reasons.)

    a) _____

    b) _____

    _____

3. What expression in paragraph 2 means "fully understand something"?

    _____

4. Who does the author criticize in paragraph 3?

_____

5. Global warming skeptics claim that global temperatures have varied throughout history and that these variations are due to natural events (and not human actions) such as solar flares. TRUE ☐ FALSE ☐

6. Why do media feature global warming skeptics? (Hint: What does the expression _stir things up_ mean in paragraph 5?)

_____

_____

_____

7. According to the author, what is the danger of believing the global warming skeptics' message?

_____

_____

8. According to the author, what is the cause of global warming?

_____

_____

9. In your own words, rewrite the quotation in paragraph 7.

_____

_____

10. Which statement best summarizes the author's main idea?
  a) Global warming must end.
  b) People must know the facts about global warming in order to stop it.
  c) It is important to understand both sides of the global warming debate.
  d) Some experts are skeptical of global warming.

Reading Discussion

▪ In small groups, discuss your answers to each of the questions below. Arrive at a group consensus.

▪ Be prepared to share your group's ideas with the rest of the class.

1. Are you interested in global warming? Explain.

2. Can we stop global warming? If so, how? If not, why not?

3. In paragraph 5, David Suzuki compares global warming skeptics to tobacco industry lobbyists. A lobbyist is someone who is paid to influence politicians on a particular issue. Is this comparison fair? Justify your response.

Word Work

In the previous section, ten new words or expressions were defined for you:

Adjectives	Expression	Noun	Verbs
1. hectic 2. riled up 3. scary	4. ~~in spite of~~	5. lack	6. debunk 7. fix 8. mislead 9. reduce 10. worry

▬ Reread the definitions provided for these words. Then reread the sentences in which the words are used to ensure you understand how each word is used in context.

▬ Fill in the blanks using the words above. Remember to conjugate the verbs as required. The first one has been done for you as an example.

1. _____*In spite of*_____ my calorie restriction and daily exercise, I gained five pounds last week.

2. Do you think that the government should _____ taxes?

3. I have a real _____ of energy; all I want to do is sleep.

4. I love _____ movies like *The Exorcist* and *The Amityville Horror*; however, after I watch them, I can't sleep!

5. In his article, David Suzuki _____ the myths surrounding global warming.

6. Most college students have _____ schedules—they study and work at the same time.

7. Most successful salespeople are honest; they never _____ their customers.

8. My DVD player is broken; I hope the technician can _____ it.

9. Sometimes I _____ about my children's future. Will they finish school? Find a job? Be happy? The concerns are endless!

10. When my neighbour parks in my parking spot, I really get _____! I have asked him many times not to do that, but he just ignores me.

Have You Heard?

For additional listening practice, visit the companion website.

melt dissolve

You will be watching two *CTV News* segments on the **melting** Arctic sea ice.

The first segment, which aired on September 28, 2005, is by Vancouver bureau chief Todd Battis. Mr. Battis's guests include: Waleed Abdalati from NASA's Cryospheric Sciences Branch, climatologist Tom Agnew from Environment Canada, Julia Langer from the World Wildlife Fund and Stéphane Dion, environment minister at the time of the report.

The second segment, which aired on May 1, 2007, is by parliamentary correspondent David Akin.

Arctic sea ice – 1979

Arctic sea ice – 2003

Pre-watching Vocabulary

Sometimes you have to understand the meaning of a *group of words* together—and not just each individual word in a group—to understand a message. Idiomatic expressions, phrasal verbs (two- or three-word verbs) and collocations (words that are frequently used together) are examples of such groups of words, generically known as expressions.

VOCABULARY TIP
When looking up expressions in a dictionary, look up one or two of the key words in the expression. You will typically find the expression defined and an example of usage given near the end of the entry. You will need a *good* dictionary for this type of exercise!

- Working with a partner, formulate ten expressions in the following exercise by correctly joining together the first and second parts of each expression. The first one has been done for you as an example.
- After verifying your answers with your teacher, write down the ten expressions on a separate sheet of paper and use a dictionary to determine their meanings.

Segment 1

First Part		Second Part
1. body of	*e*	a) apart
2. fall	____	b) on thin ice
3. ice	____	c) floes
4. tread	____	d) of life
5. web	____	e) scientific evidence

Segment 2

First Part		Second Part
6. face	____	f) rid of something
7. get	____	g) the bat
8. be a pretty	____	h) extinction
9. right off	____	i) up
10. heat	____	j) picture

LISTENING STRATEGY
Transition terms not only help you follow a writer's thoughts, but they help you follow a speaker's thoughts as well. Actively listen for the transition words used by the speakers.

While Watching

You will watch the segment twice.

- **The first time you watch, try to understand the speakers' main ideas.**
- **The second time you watch, listen for the details of what each speaker has to say, taking brief notes to help you remember the information.**

Watching Comprehension

- **Referring to your notes, respond to each of the questions below.**

Segment 1

1. How big is the polar cap?

____

2. Circle the letter(s) of the correct answer(s). More than one response is possible.

a) Arctic ice that melts in the summer no longer grows back in the winter as it used to.

b) Environment Canada Climatologist Tom Agnew predicts the Arctic Ocean will soon be ice-free.

c) We have never before had an ice-free Arctic.

3. Inuit living on the edge of the Arctic Ocean are very aware of the implications of a warming ocean. Which of the following implications is **not** mentioned in the report?
a) Bays are empty of ice.
b) The growing season is longer.
c) The permafrost is softening.
d) Hunting on ice floes is impossible.
e) Thin ice puts whalers in danger.
f) Polar bears are starving because they cannot reach their prey.
g) Birds normally confined to spots in the South are at home in the North.

4. Faced with increasing scientific evidence to the contrary, Canadian politicians can no longer dismiss global warming as a natural occurrence.   TRUE ☐   FALSE ☐

5. Which of the following statements best summarizes the main idea of the report?
a) The rapidly melting polar cap has environmental and political consequences.
b) The Inuit's traditional way of life is slowly disappearing.
c) Scientists and Inuit disagree as to the implications of a warming Arctic Ocean.
d) Global warming is caused by greenhouse gases.

Segment 2
6. How does the narrator describe sunrise "at the top of the world" (in the Arctic)?

_____

_____

7. Fill in the blanks. "The ice in the Arctic Ocean has been there, we think, for a _____ years. And so within 150 years, since the Industrial Revolution, we will have _____ _____ _____ the sea ice cover in the summer. So it's quite a drastic change."

8. A new study predicts a rapid decline in sea ice between 2030 and 2050. Explain how the disappearance of sea ice will speed up global warming.

_____

_____

9. Two consequences of the melting Arctic sea ice are mentioned in the report. The first one is provided for you. What is the second one?

a) People in some Arctic communities must move their homes so that their homes won't fall into the sea.

b) _____

10. Which of the following statements best summarizes the main idea of the report?
a) Global warming has positive and negative consequences.
b) Global warming is destroying the Arctic.
c) Arctic sea ice is melting faster than previously thought.
d) Global warming can't be stopped.

Would You Write That Down?

For additional writing practice, visit the companion website.

There are two types of writing assignments below. Free-form writing has no specific structure; essay writing does. If your teacher asks you to write an essay, be sure to respect the structure requested.

Free-form Writing

■ Write a 50- to 65-word paragraph in response to one of the following questions:

1. Do you think the world is warmer today than when you were a young child? Explain.

2. Given the greenhouse gases emitted by planes, is it acceptable to fly to a vacation destination? Justify your response.

carpool travel by car with others

3. Do you **carpool**? Why or why not?

Essay Writing

■ Write a 200- to 250-word essay on one of the thesis statements below. Your teacher may assign a thesis statement (and position) or allow you to select your own.

■ Do some research on the Internet to find evidence that supports your thesis statement. (See Appendix A on pages 178–187 to review the structure of a persuasive essay.)

1. People should (or should not) be permitted to use wood to heat their homes.

2. Air conditioners should (or should not) be banned.

3. The production of gasoline-powered vehicles should (or should not) be stopped.

4. Water consumption should (or should not) be taxed.

5. People should (or should not) act to stop global warming.

WRITING SUGGESTION
A sequencer is a special type of transition word. Examples include *first*, *second*, etc. When writing an essay, use sequencers to help the reader follow your ideas.

VOCABULARY TIP
Should is a modal, a special verb used with other verbs to express a particular mood: Eliot should study. *Should* expresses advisability or desirability. Modals are invariable: Eliza ~~shoulds~~ should do her homework.

Would You Speak Up?

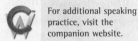

For additional speaking practice, visit the companion website.

Your teacher may ask you to participate in one or more of the following speaking activities.

Discussion

- In small groups, consider one (or more) of the following questions.
- Be prepared to share your thoughts with other groups in the class.

1. Why are many people unconcerned about global warming? Give at least two reasons.

2. Is your generation more environmentally friendly than your parents' generation? Justify your response.

3. Do you drive a car when public transportation is available? Why or why not?

4. Are you concerned by the melting of the Arctic ice? Explain.

5. What can be done to mobilize more people to take action on global warming?

SPEAKING SUGGESTION
Use transition words (*and, so, but, first, second,* etc.) when you're speaking to help the listener follow along.

Discourse

- Prepare a structured, three-minute speech on one of the thesis statements below. (See Appendix B on pages 188–190 for a suggested speaking structure.)
- Do some research to find evidence that supports your chosen thesis statement. Make sure your speech has an introduction, a development and a conclusion.

1. Car ownership should (or should not be) restricted to one car per family.

2. Sports utility vehicles (SUVs) should (or should not) be banned.

3. Global warming is (or is not) a threat to the Inuit's traditional way of life.

4. Plastic bags should (or should not) be banned.

5. Recycling is (or is not) a waste of time.

Debate

- Debate the following proposal: Actions to stop global warming are wrong. (See Appendix B on pages 190–193 for the rules of debate.)

What's That Word Mean Again?

Twenty terms were presented in this part of Unit 2: ten from the reading section and ten from the listening section. Go back and review these words and then test your vocabulary by completing the activity below.

Word Search

In the activity below, you'll be looking for the vocabulary words from Section B of this unit. Do you think you can find the words? Let's find out.

Required
• Pen or pencil

Instructions

1. For 1–10, decide which words the definitions represent, and for 11–20, decide which words are missing.

2. Find these words in the grid. (Words can go forward and backward, horizontally, vertically and diagonally.)

3. When you're finished, the first 39 unused letters in the grid will spell out a famous quotation. To uncover the quotation, pick out the letters from left to right, moving from the top line down to the bottom line.

4. Rewrite these letters, in order, in the space provided below the grid.

Definitions

1. even with (three words)

2. insufficiency

3. be concerned

4. busy

5. terrifying

6. dupe

7. enraged (two words)

8. diminish

9. refute

10. repair

11. be confronted with extinction (expression): _____ extinction

12. dispose of something (expression): _____ _____ _____ something

13. be attractive or pleasing (expression): be a _____ _____

14. instantly (expression): right _____ _____ _____

15. make (something) hot (expression): _____ _____

16. pieces of scientific proof (expression): _____ of scientific evidence

17. disintegrate (expression): _____ _____

18. floating ice (expression): _____ _____

19. be in a precarious position (expression): _____ on thin ice

20. interconnectedness of life (expression): _____ of life

C	L	P	R	E	T	T	Y	P	I	C	T	U	R	E
I	F	M	A	T	T	R	A	P	A	L	L	A	F	E
H	O	S	P	U	D	E	L	I	R	I	S	W	H	A
E	E	C	T	W	E	E	X	E	B	P	E	C	T	W
A	T	A	E	A	T	H	S	E	C	W	O	R	R	Y
T	I	R	D	E	H	R	W	E	I	U	S	W	H	A
U	P	Y	A	T	W	E	G	E	O	G	D	E	T	K
P	S	R	E	L	H	D	C	E	Q	L	T	E	C	W
K	N	K	R	M	L	M	R	T	T	B	F	A	R	T
N	I	T	T	B	I	X	X	F	I	R	L	E	Y	J
U	K	T	O	S	I	Q	P	F	Q	C	I	X	C	M
B	P	D	L	F	K	R	R	V	R	K	X	D	M	I
E	Y	E	L	Y	M	P	P	K	H	K	R	C	O	L
D	A	O	F	F	T	H	E	B	A	T	M	P	C	F
D	T	L	K	T	Q	Q	T	K	H	F	A	C	E	K

Famous quotation: _ _ _ _ _ _ _ _   _ _   _ _ _ _   _ _   _ _ _ _ _ _ _

_ _ _ _ _ _ _ _   _ _   _ _ _ _   _ _   _ _ _.

Would You Like to Work Together?

In this section, you will work with another student on a speaking project.

Project Overview

A collage is a picture made by sticking photographs, magazine or newspaper cutouts, etc., onto a surface. Collages can be constructed to make a political point. An effective collage makes audiences think and feel deeply about a given subject—graphic content is chosen for its strong visual impact. You and your partner must construct a collage that reflects *what you think* and *how you feel* about global warming. When finished, you will present your collage to the class.

Procedure

1. Work with a partner who shares your thoughts and feelings about global warming.
   Note: Your teacher may choose to assign partners.

2. Discuss your thoughts and feelings about global warming.

3. List your thoughts and feelings in point form on a separate sheet of paper. Be sure to write your names at the top of the sheet.

4. Decide what your message is.

5. Working individually, go through magazines, newspapers, etc., and cut out images that will help make your message.

6. Working together, go through the cutouts and select ten images that, when assembled, will best transmit your message.

7. On a large piece of light-coloured bristol board (56 cm x 71 cm), arrange your ten images. Note: Feel free to add graphic content (lines, arrows, etc.)—**but do not write down any words**! Let the pictures speak for themselves.

8. On the reverse side of your collage, write down ten key words that will help you present your collage—one word for each image. You may wish to use a dictionary.

9. Present your collage to your class. First describe the images, referring to key words as necessary. Second, ask members of your class to interpret your collage. (See if the message you intended to send was the one they actually received!) Finally, reveal your message to the class.

10. Graciously accept your audience's applause!

Assignment Submission
Submit your collage as well as your list of thoughts and feelings (see point 3 above) to your teacher for evaluation.

Is It Worth the Risk?

VOCABULARY TIP

Could is a modal, a special verb used with other verbs to express a particular mood: Kyle could win the grand prize. *Could* expresses possibility. Modals are invariable: Corinne ~~coulds~~ could go to the casino.

WORD CULTURE

The expression *risk life and limb* means "take a serious chance." The expression dates to the seventeenth century and, strictly speaking, makes little sense: a risk to one's life is by necessity a risk to one's arms and legs!

Everything we do in life carries a risk.

Getting out of bed in the morning is a risk: You could slip and fall on the floor!

Eating breakfast is a risk: You could choke on a piece of toast!

Despite these risks, most of us get out of bed in the morning and eat our breakfast: we calculate that the risks associated with these activities are small—and not a risk to life and limb.

The risks associated with gambling and cosmetic surgery are also small. Most Canadians gamble, but only a small number become addicts. Many Canadians have cosmetic surgery, but only a few have serious complications. Nevertheless, for those Canadians who do become addicts and for those Canadians who do have serious complications, the price paid is extremely high: some pay with their lives!

Are gambling and cosmetic surgery worth the risk?

You'll have to calculate the risks for yourself!

SECTION A
Gambling

Examines a prohibition on gambling.

SECTION B
Cosmetic Surgery

Examines physical enhancement through cosmetic surgery.

Gambling

Did You Know?

Gambling is the playing of games of chance for money.

There are many games of chance. Some of the more common ones include:
- bingo;
- lottery tickets and **raffles**;
- slot machines and video lottery terminals (VLTs);
- sports betting;
- table games, such as blackjack and poker.

raffle lottery with objects as prizes

Statistics Canada estimates that problem gamblers make up about 0.6 percent of the Canadian population and defines a problem gambler as someone who has experienced negative consequences of gambling and who gambles more than five times a year (as cited on *CBC News*).

be broke have no money

Some of the signs of problem gambling include:
- alternating between **being broke** and having lots of money;
- depression;
- difficulty sleeping;
- frequently borrowing money;
- having conflicts over money all the time;
- missing family events;

moodiness changing
temperament

- **moodiness**;
- not participating in previously enjoyed activities;

ailment mild illness

- physical **ailments** such as headaches or stomach aches;
- thinking about gambling all the time.

In 1892, the Canadian criminal code banned all gambling activities with the exception of horse racing (Stephens). Since that time, the Canadian government has gradually lifted the ban; however, some Canadians question the wisdom of legalized gambling and are calling for a return to prohibition. Below are two arguments in support of prohibition and two arguments against.

A prohibition is right because gambling:	A prohibition is wrong because gambling:
1. destroys lives.	1. is entertaining.
2. wastes money.	2. is a source of government revenue.

In this section, you will examine gambling and develop your own opinion about whether society should encourage or discourage games of chance.

What's the Buzz?

Below is a series of statements.

- Work with a partner or in small groups.
- For each statement, indicate with an "X" whether the statement is fact or fiction.
- Once you have finished, your teacher will take up the answers with you.

Fact	Statement	Fiction
☐	1. A VLT that hasn't paid out for a while is "due" to pay out.	☐
☐	2. For every dollar played on a VLT, a player will win about $0.92.	☐

Fact	Statement	Fiction
☐	3. Some numbers are drawn more frequently than others in lotteries.	☐
☐	4. The more you gamble, the more you increase your **odds** of winning the money played.	☐
☐	5. Your odds of winning the grand prize in the Super 7 lottery are 1 in 20,963,833.	☐

odds chances

Source: lotoquebec.com

Discussion

- Working with a partner or in a small group, discuss and respond to the questions below.
- Be prepared to share your responses with the class.

1. Do you buy lottery tickets? Why or why not?

2. If you won the grand prize in a lottery, would you want others to know? Why or why not?

3. "The love of money is the root of all evil" is a common English proverb. What does this proverb mean? Do you agree with it?

Have You Read?

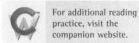
For additional reading practice, visit the companion website.

Brian Williams is the city editor of the *Guelph Mercury*, the newspaper in which his article "Bad Poker Night Curbed My Enthusiasm" appeared on December 1, 2006.

Before Reading

- Remember to skim and scan: read the defined words and comprehension questions before you read the article.

READING STRATEGY
When doing an assigned reading, think about why the teacher has assigned the reading. This will help you focus your attention on the task at hand. A focused reader is an effective reader.

While Reading

Brian Williams' article is interesting to read because he uses anecdotes to make his point. Enjoy the stories, but don't lose sight of the author's main point. Ask yourself why the author is telling you the stories.

BAD POKER NIGHT CURBED MY ENTHUSIASM

BY BRIAN WILLIAMS

Gambling addiction thankfully is not something I have ever had to battle, but I can sure see how young people **get hooked**.

The desire to be cool and follow the crowd can keep you from being the one who says he's not interested in playing games for money.

5 I flirted with the concept of playing for money when I was a teenager. I **recall** the thrill of winning even a small amount and the lure of playing again to win more.

It started on the golf course. Once introduced to the concept, it seemed we couldn't tee it up without playing for money, almost as if not doing so
10 meant we were **wasting our** time being on the course. A couple of **bucks** here, a couple there led to side bets and games within games and before you knew it, a bad round left you twenty dollars poorer.

That doesn't sound like a great deal of cash, but that was more than twenty years ago and if it happened often enough it could sure eat into the
15 paycheque from your part-time job.

get hooked become addicted

recall remember

waste time not use time well

buck dollar (slang)

And it didn't stop once we walked off the golf course. Board games would be played for money, a trip or two to the harness races resulted in minor gains and then eventually the playing cards came out. But I only took part in a couple of poker nights because I learned my lesson the night I lost
20 eighty dollars.

cure heal

In terms of gambling, it was probably the best eighty dollars I ever spent because it **cured** me.

Much is being made these days of getting the word out to teens about the dangers of gambling. The popularity of poker is seen as a big contributor
appealing tempting
25 to the problem, made even more **appealing** by the seemingly endless hours of television coverage of people playing for big money.

The Responsible Gambling Council says people eighteen to twenty-four have the highest rates of gambling problems in Ontario. Another group, the Centre for Addiction and Mental Health, says eighty percent of high school students have gambled at least once in the past year. I'd be willing
bet gamble
30 to **bet** it's unlikely those who did gamble limited themselves to one time only.

A story in the *Mercury* last month told the story of University of Guelph student Mark Zettel. He started playing poker for fun in high school and
35 ended up spending five or six hours a night playing online.

He said he ended up winning thousands of dollars, making it better than a part-time job to help pay for school and allowing him to buy toys such as a motorcycle.

But it turned out to be "a hard way to make an easy living." In the summer
40 he started to back away from the online game, saying he became tired of
moody irritable
feeling distracted and **moody** when he was losing.

"I'd wake up in the morning and the first thing I wanted to do is play," he said last month. "It's probably not the best thing to do."

glad happy

All I know is I'm **glad** we didn't have the Internet when I was a teenager.
45 The lure of the online poker sites, along with a good number of friends who would likely be playing, probably wouldn't have been a good combination for me.

hurt damage

And if all the transactions are electronic, just numbers on a computer screen, I wonder if it would **hurt** as much right at the time of losing as it
50 did the day I had to hand over that cold, hard cash.

593 words

Reading Comprehension

■ Respond to each of the questions.

1. While the author has never had a gambling problem, he understands how young people become addicts.

TRUE ☐ FALSE ☐

2. According to the author, why do young people gamble? List two reasons.

a) _____

b) _____

3. What game introduced the author to gambling?

_____

4. What other games did the author later bet on? List three.

a) _____

b) _____

c) _____

5. In your own words, why did the author stop gambling?

_____

_____

6. According to the author, what is aggravating the teen gambling problem?

_____

_____

7. What age group is most affected by gambling problems?

_____

8. How many hours a day did Mark Zettel spend playing online poker?

_____

9. Why did Mark Zettel start to limit his online gambling?

_____

_____

_____

10. What is the main idea of Mr. Williams's article?
   a) Poker is addictive.
   b) People always lose money when gambling.
   c) It is increasingly important for teenagers to be informed about the dangers of gambling.
   d) Teenagers should not be allowed to gamble.

Reading Discussion

- In small groups, discuss your answers to each of the questions.
- Be prepared to share your group's ideas with the rest of the class.

1. In your opinion, why do young people gamble?

2. Do you gamble? If so, how do you feel when you win? When you lose? If you don't gamble, why not?

3. In your opinion, is online poker more addictive than offline poker (a game of poker with players sitting around a table)? Why or why not? Note: You might want to reread the last paragraph of the article for Brian Williams's opinion on the subject.

Word Work

In the previous section, ten new terms were defined for you.

Adjectives	Expressions	Noun	Verbs
1. appealing 2. glad 3. moody	4. ~~get hooked~~ 5. waste time	6. buck	7. bet 8. cure 9. hurt 10. recall

- In the text that follows, there are ten terms in italics. Replace each of the terms with one of the terms from the list above.
- If you're replacing a verb, be sure to conjugate correctly. Pluralize nouns if required. The first one has been done for you as an example.

I *was addicted* (¹._____*got hooked*_____) from the very start.

As I *remember* (²._____), it was my very first visit to the casino, and I had only put a couple of nickels in a slot machine when I won the jackpot: a hundred *dollars* (³._____)!

At that point, I was still thinking clearly. I remember telling myself: quit while you're ahead; take your money and go home.

But I wouldn't listen to reason: winning "easy money" was quite *tempting* (⁴._____).

I took that hundred dollars and "invested" it in another machine. This time, I wasn't playing for nickels; I was playing for dimes.

As easily as I had won the hundred dollars, I lost it. At the time, I was *happy* (⁵._____) I had brought my debit card with me. I withdrew fifty dollars from my account, and decided to change machines: I moved to the quarter machines, and continued losing. I had a sick feeling in the pit of my stomach and was feeling rather *irritable* (⁶._____).

I went back to the automatic teller and withdrew another fifty dollars, which I lost as quickly as the previous fifty. Several hours passed, and by the time I finally left the casino, I had *gambled* (⁷._____) and lost more than two hundred dollars.

When I arrived home, I was rude to my roommate. My actions that night severely *damaged* (⁸._____) our relationship.

I foolishly went back to the casino the following evening, determined to win back my losses. I *did not use my time well* (9._____): I lost another two hundred dollars.

The next night I returned once again to the scene of the crime. Unfortunately, that night I was a "winner": I "won" three hundred dollars (conveniently forgetting that overall, I was "down" about a hundred dollars).

To this day, I am convinced that a third loss in a row would have *healed* (10._____) me of my gambling addiction.

Sometimes you have to lose in order to win!

Have You Heard?

For additional listening practice, visit the companion website.

You will be watching two *CTV News* video segments on gambling.

In the first segment, which aired on October 3, 2003, reporter Geneviève Beauchemin examines the possible link between suicide and gambling. Featured guests include the director of the International Centre for Youth Gambling, Dr. Jeff Derevensky, and Phyllis Vineberg, whose son Trevor ended his life due to problem gambling.

In the second segment, which aired on April 8, 2001, reporter Cory Atkins interviews teens who frequent casinos. Featured guests include a group of teenagers, Dr. Jeff Derevensky and several individuals from the Canadian Foundation on Compulsive Gambling.

Pre-watching Vocabulary

The following is a list of five terms used in video segment 1 and five terms used in video segment 2:

Segment 1	Segment 2
• addictive (adj.) • ~~commit suicide~~ (exp.) • entertainment (n.) • increase (v.) • sin (n.)	• be in debt (exp.) • betting (n.) • broke (adj.) • disorder (n.) • play (n.)

■ Working alone or with a partner, write each term beside its proper definition in the space provided. The first term has been done for you as an example.

Segment 1

Definitions	Terms
1. end one's life	*commit suicide (exp.)*
2. creating a dependence	
3. transgression of moral law	
4. enlarge or augment	
5. activity which amuses or diverts	

Segment 2

Definitions	Terms
6. gambling	
7. production or a show	
8. sickness	
9. owe money	
10. having no money	

WORD CULTURE
The expression *to bet one's bottom dollar* is used to express complete certainty about something: When asked if there would be snow for Christmas, the meteorologist said she was willing to bet her bottom dollar.

While Watching

You will watch each video segment twice.

- Before watching the first time, read through the comprehension questions below.
- Take notes as you watch and then respond to the comprehension questions.

Segment 1

1. What two adjectives does Phyllis Vineberg use to describe video lottery terminals (VLTs)?

a) _____

b) _____

2. Fill in the blanks. "The latest numbers show one addict _____ _____ every two weeks. Five times as many as five years ago." (Beauchemin)

3. Which of the following statements is **false**?
a) The link between suicide and gambling is hard to establish.
b) In Canada, the number of suicides linked to gambling is increasing.
c) The number of suicides linked to gambling is decreasing in Nova Scotia.
d) Canadians no longer perceive of gambling as wrong.

4. How many VLTs are there in Québec? _____

5. What is the main idea of the report?
a) Most problem gamblers commit suicide.
b) Gambling related suicide is a growing problem in Canada.
c) VLTs should be banned from school zones.
d) VLTs are addictive, especially for teenagers.

Segment 2

6. What two reasons do the teens give for going to the casino on a Saturday night?

a) _____

b) _____

7. According to gambling expert Jeff Derevensky, gambling is now more popular with high school teenagers than smoking, drinking alcohol or doing drugs.   TRUE ☐ FALSE ☐

8. Fill in the blanks. "There are now more legalized gambling venues across the country. And studies have shown that as the number of places to gamble _____, so does the number of people placing bets—especially young people. They are four times more likely to have gambling _____ than adults."

LISTENING STRATEGY
Communication is both verbal and nonverbal. Understanding nonverbal communication (or body language) is helpful in understanding the speaker's message. Watch student Anthony Crawford's body language as he talks about his gambling losses.

9. Which of the following statements is **false**?
   a) Actors from The Canadian Foundation on Compulsive Gambling will perform their anti-gambling play at more than 150 high schools.
   b) The earlier people start gambling, the more likely they are to have a problem later on.
   c) The anonymous young man interviewed for the segment is more than $25,000 in debt.
   d) Casinos discourage problem gamblers from gambling.

10. What is the main idea of the report?
    a) Teenagers should be barred from casinos.
    b) Teenagers are ignoring society's anti-gambling message.
    c) Most teenagers gamble regularly.
    d) Problem teenage gambling is on the increase.

Would You Write That Down?

For additional writing practice, visit the companion website.

Your teacher may ask you to complete one or both of the writing activities below. If asked to write an essay, be sure to structure your writing clearly.

Free-form Writing

■ Write a 50- to 65-word paragraph in response to one of the following questions:

1. Why does the government build casinos?

2. Do you think you could ever become addicted to gambling? Explain.

3. Is playing poker for fun as interesting as playing poker for money? Why or why not?

WRITING SUGGESTION
When writing an essay, avoid unnecessary structures like "I think that ..." and "I feel that ...." Because it's *your* essay, the readers already know they're reading about *your* thoughts and *your* feelings.

Essay Writing

■ Write a 200- to 250-word essay on one of the thesis statements below. Your teacher may assign a thesis statement (and position) or allow you to select your own.

■ Do some research on the Internet to find evidence that supports your thesis statement. (See Appendix A on pages 178–187 to review the structure of a persuasive essay.)

1. Money can (or cannot) buy happiness.

2. Young people do (or do not) need to be protected from gambling.

3. Sports betting should (or should not) be prohibited.

4. The government should (or should not) pay for gambling addiction treatment.

5. A problem gambler can (or cannot) be cured.

Would You Speak Up?

Your teacher may ask you to participate in one or more of the following speaking activities.

For additional speaking practice, visit the companion website.

Discussion

- In small groups, consider one (or more) of the following questions.
- Be prepared to share your thoughts with other groups in the class.

1. Are some numbers lucky and other numbers unlucky? Explain.

2. Should casinos be allowed to operate twenty-four hours a day, seven days a week? Why or why not?

3. Should people under the age of eighteen be allowed to buy lottery tickets? Justify your response.

4. In Brian William's article "Bad Poker Night Curbed My Enthusiasm," the author implies that young people gamble to be "cool." In your opinion, is gambling cool?

5. Studies indicate that more men than women have a gambling problem. Why do you think this is?

Discourse

- Prepare a structured, three-minute speech on one of the thesis statements below. (See Appendix B on pages 188–190 for a suggested discourse structure.)
- Do some research to find evidence that supports your chosen thesis statement.
- Make sure your speech has an introduction, a development and a conclusion.

1. Gambling is (or is not) a harmless pastime.

2. TV poker shows should (or should not) be banned.

3. The legal gambling age should (or should not) be raised from 18 to 21.

4. VLTs should (or should not) be banned from school zones.

5. Gambling is (or is not) a waste of money.

Debate

- Debate the following proposal: A prohibition on gambling is wrong. (See Appendix B on pages 190–193 for the rules of debate.)

What's That Word Mean Again?

Now it's time to review the vocabulary terms studied in the reading and the listening sections of this part of the unit. Twenty terms were presented. Do you still remember them? Let's find out.

Crossword Puzzle

A crossword puzzle is a good way to review vocabulary.

Required
• Pen or pencil

Instructions
Read the clues on the following page and fill in the corresponding blanks below.

Across	Down
1. happy (adj.)	**2.** create a dependence (adj.)
4. production or a show (n.)	**3.** heal (v.)
7. damage (v.)	**5.** tempting (adj.)
8. get _____: expression meaning "to be addicted"	**6.** having no money (adj.)
	9. sickness (n.)
10. be in _____: expression meaning "to owe money"	**13.** gamble (v.)
11. _____ time: expression meaning "to not use time well"	**14.** _____ suicide: expression meaning "to end one's life"
12. transgression of a moral law (n.)	**15.** enlarge or augment (v.)
16. gambling (n.)	**16.** dollar (n.)
17. irritable (adj.)	
18. remember (v.)	
19. activity which amuses or diverts (n.)	

Would You Like to Work Together?

In this section, you are asked to work with another student on a writing project.

Project Overview

sample test group

An opinion poll is an investigation of public opinion. A **sample** of a given population is questioned and, if the sample is representative, the results are applied to the population as a whole. For this project, you are going to conduct an opinion poll on gambling.

Types of Questions

Questions can be divided into two types: open- and close-ended. Open-ended questions are questions to which there is more than one answer: How do you feel about gambling? Close-ended questions are questions to which there are a finite number of answers: Should the government operate casinos? (The answer is either "yes" or "no.") In this project, you will use close-ended questions as the answers are easier to analyze. The following are examples of close-ended questions frequently found in opinion polls:

Categorical

Circle one: male / female

Multiple Choice

How often do you gamble? Circle one answer:
a) once a year or less   **c)** once a month   **e)** once a week
b) several times a year   **d)** several times a month   **f)** several times a week

Likert Scale

How important is gambling to you? Circle one answer:

1	**2**	**3**	**4**	**5**
not important at all	somewhat important	unsure	very important	extremely important

Ordinal

Write a number between 1 and 5 beside each of the items below. Put a "1" next to the item that is **most** important to you personally, a "2" beside the item that is **second most** important to you personally, etc.

_____ **a)** spending time with friends   _____ **d)** studying

_____ **b)** gambling   _____ **e)** playing sports

_____ **c)** working

Writing and Conducting an Opinion Poll

Working with your assigned (or chosen) partner:

1. Create ten questions on gambling. Important: Your first two questions should determine the gender and age of the respondents.

2. Submit your proposed questions to your teacher. Your teacher will correct any grammar or spelling errors and may suggest replacing or reordering certain questions.

3. Type your corrected list of questions, adding the following:
   a) A title: Opinion Poll on Gambling
   b) Introductory instructions: Please respond to each of the ten questions below. Answering the questions will only take a few minutes. Your participation is voluntary. The results of the poll will be presented to my English teacher as part of a class project; the results may be discussed in class. Your confidentiality will be respected. Do not write your name.

4. Print out ten copies of your opinion poll, one for each participant in your survey.

5. Find ten people willing to complete your poll.

6. Compile your results.

Compiling the Results

When compiling the results:

1. Describe the sample.
   Example: *Ten teenagers—seven males and three females, studying in humanities at the Bois-de-Boulogne college in Montreal—responded to the poll.*

2. For each question, indicate the breakdown of the responses.
   Example: *Three respondents indicated that they gambled "once a year or less."*

3. Draw conclusions.
   Example: *In general, gambling does not appear to be a problem for the students polled.*
   Note: Due to the sample size, findings cannot be generalized to a given population.

4. Include an example of the opinion poll distributed. Do not include the actual polls completed: dispose of these polls in a manner that respects the respondents' confidentiality (shredding, etc.).

Submit your assignment to your teacher for evaluation.

Cosmetic Surgery

Did You Know?

Plastic surgery can be divided into two categories:

1. Reconstructive surgery
2. Cosmetic surgery

defect imperfection
enhance improve

The objective of reconstructive surgery is to repair a **defect** or an injury while the objective of cosmetic surgery is to **enhance** a person's appearance.

Some of the more common cosmetic surgery procedures include:
- botox injections
- breast implants
- buttocks augmentation
- chemical peels

facelift surgical procedure to remove facial lines

- **facelifts**
- hair replacement
- liposuction
- microdermabrasion
- neck tucks

tummy stomach (informal)

- nose jobs
- **tummy** tucks

hush-hush confidential (informal)

In the recent past, cosmetic surgery was reserved almost exclusively for the rich and famous and was quite **hush-hush**. This is no longer the case. Today, ordinary people are having cosmetic surgery and most are happy to talk about it. While some see cosmetic surgery as a method of self-improvement, others see it as an expression of vanity—and a risky one at that! Below are two arguments in support of physical enhancement through cosmetic surgery, and two arguments against.

Physical enhancement through cosmetic surgery is right because it:	Physical enhancement through cosmetic surgery is wrong because it:
1. helps people feel better about themselves.	1. is unnatural.
2. helps people surmount genetic barriers to beauty.	2. is risky.

In this section, you will examine cosmetic surgery and decide for yourself whether beauty is worth any cost.

What's the Buzz?

Below is a series of statements.

- Work with a partner or in small groups.
- For each statement, indicate with an "X" whether the statement is fact or fiction.
- Once you have finished, your teacher will take up the answers with you.

scar mark on skin

Fact	Statement	Fiction
☐	1. All cosmetic surgeries leave visible **scars**.	☐
☐	2. In the United States, liposuction is the most common cosmetic surgery procedure.	☐
☐	3. It can take up to a year for a scar to heal.	☐
☐	4. Liposuction is an easy way to lose weight.	☐
☐	5. Not all cosmetic surgery brings risk.	☐

Discussion

- Working with a partner or in a small group, discuss and respond to the questions below.
- Be prepared to share your responses with the class.

1. Would you ever have cosmetic surgery? Why or why not?

2. Are attractive people happier than unattractive people? Explain.

3. "Beauty is only skin deep" is a common English proverb. What does this proverb mean? Do you agree with it?

Have You Read?

For additional reading practice, visit the companion website.

Ashley Bursey is a writer whose article "Waiting a Lifetime for Plastic Surgery" appeared in the *New Brunswick Telegraph-Journal* on March 31, 2007.

READING STRATEGY
When doing an assigned reading, think about why the teacher has assigned the reading. This will help you focus your attention on the task at hand. A focused reader is an effective reader.

Before Reading

- Remember to skim and scan: read the defined words and comprehension questions before you read the article.

It's like looking in a mirror!

While Reading

Ashley Bursey's article is interesting to read because she uses an anecdote to make her point. Enjoy the story, but don't lose sight of the author's main point. Ask yourself why the author is telling you the story.

WAITING A LIFETIME FOR PLASTIC SURGERY

BY ASHLEY BURSEY

gag joke

So I'm riffling through the pages of a women's mag[1] when I come across something so scary that at first I think it must be some kind of joke. A **gag**, perhaps. A mockery of today's superficial society.

peek look
ad advertisement

Another **peek** at the page assures me I am, unfortunately, wrong. Days
5 later, I see the **ad** again in another magazine.

frightening terrifying

"What is it?" you ask. Surely it can't be more **frightening** than those skeletal models in diet pill ads. Think again. It's an ad for cosmetic surgery, which itself isn't too terrifying. It's the slogan that runs along with it that worries me.

10 We see two attractive, middle-aged women wearing big smiles and fashionable clothing. They're dining at a fancy restaurant—because that's where all the pretty, wrinkle-free people dine, I guess—and holding menus that tell readers to seize the day and get cosmetic surgery. Because, as the ad puts it, "We've been waiting long enough." The wrinkle-free faces

cheerful joyful

15 of these **cheerful** ladies are **eerie**, but it's the message that's even scarier.

eerie weird

I'm all for makeup. I love a great liquid liner or new bronzer. But makeup is makeup. Injecting your body with chemicals is a whole other kettle of fish. The ad fails to mention in its big, bouncy letters that these chemicals can cause serious heart problems or allergic reactions.

erase remove

20 There's something more than a little off-putting about this idea of **erasing** nature's effects in favour of an ideal; a fabrication of the face. It's a mask, almost, an unlined shell with plump lips, smooth forehead and eyes free of laugh lines. Whatever happened to aging gracefully? This glossy piece of slick advertising tells me I can essentially stop the clock, for a few easy
25 payments.

Well, I'm sick of it. I'm sick of people turning to cosmetic surgery because they need to look like everyone else. I'm sick of the guessing game the tabloids play: "Whose boobs[2] are these?" or "What happened to Ashlee's nose?" But most of all, I'm sick of people feeling inferior because they've
30 lived life and no longer have the Barbie-doll figure they did when they were seventeen. There's a reason she's Barbie, folks—she's plastic.

famous well known

I'm a fan of some of the counter-ads out there. There are cosmetics companies—one **famous** soap company in particular—that feature happy, realistic women in their ads. Ladies with grey hair, laugh lines and imper-
35 fect teeth. When you look at someone so real, so full of life, it's impossible not to see her beauty.

wrinkle facial line
eagerly enthusiastically

The Sophia Lorens of the world—the timeless beauties who aren't afraid to sport a **wrinkle** or two—are the real role models. That's why it's so sad to hear of ten-year-olds who would **eagerly** jump under the knife. Or
40 about the perverse attraction of *The Swan*,[3] the cut'em-up slasher show that rivalled *Friday the 13th* for its slicing and dicing.

I don't want to open a magazine and be faced with these imperfectly perfect faces looking out from ads that tell me that, in order to feel like I'm worth anything, I have to inject chemicals in my lips, smooth my forehead, fix my nose or pad my cheeks. Sorry, but no thanks.

The ad tells me this is my time. If that's true, why would I waste it turning myself into someone else?

567 words

1. Magazine
2. Slang term for breasts
3. American reality show in which women have their appearance drastically changed by cosmetic surgery

Reading Comprehension

▬ Respond to each of the questions.

1. In line 1, the author uses the verb *riffle*. Without using a dictionary, what do you think this verb means?

_____

_____

_____

2. How many times does the author look at the ad for cosmetic surgery?

_____

_____

_____

_____

3. The author equates using makeup with having plastic surgery. Hint: The expression *a whole other kettle of fish* means "something completely different."   TRUE ☐ FALSE ☐

4. According to the author, what are two possible consequences of injecting one's body with chemicals to remove wrinkles?

a) _____

b) _____

5. The author equates cosmetic surgery done on the face with lying.   TRUE ☐ FALSE ☐

6. According to the author, why do people have cosmetic surgery? List two reasons.

a) _____

b) _____

7. In your own words, what is a "counter-ad"?

_____

_____

8. The author looks upon beautiful older women who have not had cosmetic surgery as role models.   TRUE ☐   FALSE ☐

9. According to the author, what message is the message of cosmetic surgery?

_____

_____

10. What is the main idea of Ms. Bursey's article?
   a) Cosmetic surgery is wrong.
   b) Ads for cosmetic surgery should be banned.
   c) True beauty is based on being oneself and accepting one's age.
   d) Children as young as ten years old are having plastic surgery.

Reading Discussion

- In small groups, discuss your answers to each of the questions below. Try to arrive at a group consensus.
- Be prepared to share your group's ideas with the rest of the class.

1. Is a woman in her eighties beautiful? Is a man in his eighties handsome? Justify your answers.

2. Do you agree or disagree with the following statement: Wrinkles make a man look "distinguished," but they make a woman look "old." Explain your point of view.

3. How do you feel about a middle-aged woman dyeing her hair? A middle-aged man?

VOCABULARY TIP
Typically the adjective *beautiful* is reserved for women, and the adjective *handsome* is reserved for men: That beautiful woman married a handsome man.

Word Work

In the previous section, ten terms were defined for you:

Adjectives	Adverb	Nouns	Verb
1. cheerful	5. eagerly	6. ad	10. erase
2. eerie		7. gag	
3. ~~famous~~		8. peek	
4. frightening		9. wrinkle	

- In the text on page 72, there are ten terms in italics. Replace each of the terms with one of the terms from the list above.
- If you're replacing a verb, be sure to conjugate correctly. Pluralize nouns if required. The first one has been done for you as an example.

A couple of months ago, my friends and I gathered around the TV to watch an action movie starring a *well-known* (1. _____*famous*_____) Hollywood actor. For months, we had *enthusiastically* (2. _____) been waiting for the film to be released on DVD.

While I enjoyed the film, I found myself somewhat distracted by the middle-aged actor's face, a "perfect face" without a single *facial line* (3. _____) from which all expression seemed to have been *removed* (4. _____). The overall effect was *weird* (5. _____) and more than a little disconcerting. As a *joke* (6. _____), I mentioned to my friends that I was thinking of getting a facelift and to my dismay, nobody tried to talk me out of it!

The next day, I noticed an *advertisement* (7. _____) for cosmetic surgery in the local paper. The advertisement was for a clinic not too far from my home, so I called the clinic and set up a consultation. When I arrived for my appointment, an irritatingly *joyful* (8. _____) receptionist welcomed me and sent me to the waiting room to fill out a few forms. What I saw in the waiting room was *terrifying* (9. _____): the room was filled with people in various stages of mummification! One of the guys looked like a character straight out of *The Mummy*! I tried not to stare but every once in a while, I had to take a quick *look* (10. _____).

When I got home that evening, I took a good look at myself in the mirror and saw a middle-aged man with sagging skin, wrinkles and a double chin. What I saw distressed me, but my reflection seemed much less distressing than what I had seen in the waiting room earlier that day.

While I haven't fully accepted the changes time has made to my face, I am not quite ready to join the cast of *The Mummy Returns*! For now, the surgeon's knife will just have to wait.

Have You Heard?

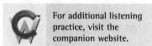

For additional listening practice, visit the companion website.

In January 2007, the CBC radio program *World Report* ran a series entitled "Fountain of Youth." You are about to listen to two segments from this series. Host Judy Maddren introduces the reports filed by Frank Koller. In segment 1, Mr. Koller's guests include Dr. Peter Brownrigg, career counsellor Ken Zaborniak and Wesleyan University Professor Tanya Rosenblat. In segment 2, his guests include adult students from the Algonquin Careers Academy Pharmacy Assistant Program in Ottawa, Tanya Rosenblat and University of Pennsylvania Economist Andrew Postlewaite. Both segments aired on January 9, 2007.

Pre-listening Vocabulary

The following is a list of five terms used in radio segment 1 and five terms used in radio segment 2:

Segment 1	Segment 2
• attractiveness (n.) • competitive edge (exp.) • jaw (n.) • plain (adj.) • ~~skill~~ (n.)	• boom (n.) • bias (n.) • height (n.) • link (n.) • wage (n.)

■ Working alone or with a partner, write each term beside its proper definition in the space provided. The first term has been done for you as an example.

Segment 1

Definitions	Terms
1. ability	*skill*
2. bone in which teeth are set	
3. business advantage	
4. pleasant appearance	
5. unattractive	

Segment 2

Definitions	Terms
6. connection	
7. payment for work	
8. prejudice	
9. significant increase	
10. stature	

While Listening

- You will listen to each radio segment from *World Report*'s "Fountain of Youth" twice. Before listening the first time, read through the comprehension questions below.
- Take notes as you listen and then respond to the comprehension questions.

Segment 1

1. Fill in the blanks. "Many people will take a course or learn a new _____ to increase their paycheque, but getting a facelift may also work." (Maddren)

2. Facial plastic surgeon Dr. Peter Brownrigg claims that the motivation of many of his new patients has changed in the last ten years. How has their motivation changed?

   _____

   _____

3. Which of the following statements is **false**? Ken Zaborniak:
   a) works in Ottawa.
   b) had a neck tuck in Puerto Rico.
   c) had an accident with his car.
   d) thinks plastic surgery is good for business.

4. Professor Tanya Rosenblat claims that physical attractiveness matters only in occupations where there is a lot of interaction between workers and customers.   TRUE ☐ FALSE ☐

5. What is the main idea of the report?
   a) More and more men are having facial plastic surgery.
   b) More and more employees are having plastic surgery as it is increasingly financially advantageous to look younger and better in the workplace.
   c) An employee's physical attractiveness is more important to employers than his (or her) abilities.
   d) Younger employees are earning more money than older employees.

WORD CULTURE
Juan Ponce de León (1460-1521) was a Spanish explorer who attempted to find the mythical Fountain of Youth in an area of the world known today as Florida.

LISTENING STRATEGY
Listening to audio segments requires more concentration than watching video segments, as understanding relies on verbal communication alone; nonverbal clues are absent. You may wish to close your eyes or stare at a blank surface as you're listening to the segments to optimize your level of concentration.

Segment 2

6. According to host Judy Maddren, what two reasons partially explain the recent increase in the number of workers having plastic surgery?

   a) _____

   b) _____

7. Adult students graduating from the Algonquin Careers Academy doubt that physical attractiveness affects employment opportunities and salary levels.

   TRUE ☐   FALSE ☐

8. According to Professor Tanya Rosenblat, how much more do good-looking (and younger) employees earn than their average-looking (and older) counterparts?

   _____

9. Economist Andrew Postlewaite claims that taller people earn more than their shorter counterparts.

   TRUE ☐   FALSE ☐

10. Which statement best summarizes the main idea of the report?
    a) Looks and age count in the business world.
    b) Experts and non-experts disagree on the importance of looks in the workplace.
    c) Good-looking employees get promoted faster than average-looking employees.
    d) Employees can change their appearance, but they cannot change their stature.

Would You Write That Down?

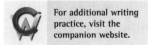

For additional writing practice, visit the companion website.

Your teacher may ask you to complete one or both of the writing activities below. If asked to write an essay, be sure to structure your writing clearly.

Free-form Writing

■ Write a 50- to 65-word paragraph in response to one of the following questions:

1. Would you ever consider having cosmetic surgery? Why or why not?

2. Do people look better or worse after a facelift? Explain.

3. Is it socially acceptable to be "old" in our society? Justify your position.

Essay Writing

- Write a 200- to 250-word essay on one of the thesis statements below. Your teacher may assign a thesis statement (and position) or allow you to select your own.
- Do some research on the Internet to find evidence that supports your thesis statement. (See Appendix A on pages 178–187 to review the structure of a persuasive essay.)

1. Brains are (or are not) more important than beauty.

minor somebody who is not an adult

2. **Minors** should (or should not) be allowed to have cosmetic surgery.

3. Society places (does not place) too much importance on appearance.

4. Short people are (or are not) discriminated against in the workplace.

5. Obese people are (or are not) discriminated against in today's society.

> WRITING SUGGESTION
> When writing an essay, avoid unnecessary structures like "I think that …" and "I feel that …." Because it's *your* essay, the readers already know they're reading about *your* thoughts and *your* feelings.

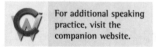

Would You Speak Up?

For additional speaking practice, visit the companion website.

Your teacher may ask you to participate in one or more of the following speaking activities.

Discussion

- In small groups, consider one (or more) of the following questions.
- Be prepared to share your thoughts with other groups in the class.

1. In English, there is a well-known saying that "beauty is in the eye of the beholder." In your own words, what does this saying mean?

date go out with

2. Who would you rather **date**? Someone who is attractive but uninteresting or someone who is unattractive but interesting? Explain your choice.

3. Why do more women have cosmetic surgery than men?

4. Make a list of the world's five most beautiful women. What do these women have in common? List a minimum of five traits.

5. Make a list of the world's five most handsome men. What do these men have in common? List a minimum of five traits.

Discourse

- Prepare a structured, three-minute speech on one of the thesis statements below. (See Appendix B on pages 188–190 for a suggested discourse structure.)
- Do some research to find evidence that supports your chosen thesis statement.
- Make sure your speech has an introduction, a development and a conclusion.

1. Women are (or are not) more concerned about their appearance than men.

2. Unattractive people are (or are not) discriminated against.

3. Cosmetic surgery is (or is not) risky.

4. People should (or should not) dye their hair to look younger.

5. Cosmetic surgery is (or is not) a waste of money.

PRONUNCIATION TIP
The plural form of *woman* is *women*, pronounced as "wimmin."

Debate

- Debate the following proposal: physical enhancement through cosmetic surgery is wrong. (See Appendix B on pages 190–193 for the rules of debate.)

What's That Word Mean Again?

Now it's time to review the vocabulary terms studied in the reading and the listening sections of this part of the unit. Twenty terms were presented. Do you still remember them? Let's find out.

Crossword Puzzle

A crossword puzzle is a good way to review vocabulary.

Required
• Pen or pencil

Instructions
Read the clues and fill in the corresponding blanks on the following page.

Across

1. enthusiastically (adv.)
4. joyful (adj.)
5. look (n.)
8. advertisement (n.)
11. terrifying (adj.)
14. facial line (n.)
15. remove (v.)
18. connection (n.)
19. well-known (adj.)
20. unattractive (adj.)

Down

2. pleasant appearance (n.)
3. stature (n.)
6. weird (adj.)
7. payment for work (n.)
9. prejudice (n.)
10. bone in which teeth are set (n.)
12. joke (n.)
13. competitive _____; expression meaning "business advantage"
16. ability (n.)
17. significant increase (n.)

Would You Like to Work Together?

In this section, you are asked to work with another student on a writing project.

sample test group

Project Overview
An opinion poll is an investigation of public opinion. A **sample** of a given population is questioned and, if the sample is representative, the results are applied to the population as a whole. For this project, you are going to conduct an opinion poll on attitudes toward cosmetic surgery.

Types of Questions
Questions can be divided into two types: open- and close-ended. Open-ended questions are questions to which there is more than one answer: How do you feel about cosmetic surgery? Close-ended questions are questions to which there are a finite number of answers: Should young teenagers be allowed to have cosmetic surgery? (The answer is either "yes" or "no.") In this project, you will use close-ended questions as the answers are easier to analyze. The following are examples of close-ended questions frequently found in opinion polls:

Categorical

Circle one: male / female

Multiple Choice

How many people do you know personally who have had a cosmetic procedure?
Circle one answer.

a) none	**c)** two	**e)** four
b) one	**d)** three	**f)** five or more

Likert Scale

When choosing a "significant other," how important are looks to you?
Circle one answer.

1	**2**	**3**	**4**	**5**
not important at all	somewhat important	unsure	very important	extremely important

---

Ordinal

Write a number between 1 and 5 beside each of the items below. Put a "1" next to the item that is **most** important to you personally, a "2" beside the item that is **second most** important to you personally, etc.

_____ **a)** health	_____ **d)** kindness
_____ **b)** beauty	_____ **e)** generosity
_____ **c)** intelligence	

Writing and Conducting an Opinion Poll

Working with your assigned (or chosen) partner:

1. Create ten questions on cosmetic surgery. Important: Your first two questions should determine the gender and age of the respondents.

2. Submit your proposed questions to your teacher. Your teacher will correct any grammar or spelling errors and may suggest replacing or reordering certain questions.

3. Type your corrected list of questions, adding the following:
   a) A title: Opinion Poll on Cosmetic Surgery
   b) Introductory instructions: Please respond to each of the ten questions below. Answering the questions will only take a few minutes. Your participation is voluntary. The results of the poll will be presented to my English teacher as part of a class project; the results may be discussed in class. Your confidentiality will be respected. Do not write your name.

4. Print out ten copies of your opinion poll, one for each participant in your survey.

5. Find ten people willing to complete your poll.

6. Compile your results.

Compiling the Results

When compiling the results:

1. Describe the sample.
   Example: *Ten teenagers—seven males and three females, studying in science at the Bois-de-Boulogne college in Montreal—responded to the poll.*

2. For each question, indicate the breakdown of the responses.
   Example: *Three respondents indicated that they personally knew five or more people who had had a cosmetic procedure.*

3. Draw conclusions.
   Example: *In general, physical appearance seems to be very important in the choice of a "significant other."*
   Note: Due to the sample size, findings cannot be generalized to a given population.

4. Include an example of the opinion poll distributed. Do not include the actual polls completed: dispose of these polls in a manner which respects the respondents' confidentiality (shredding, etc.).

Submit your assignment to your teacher for evaluation.

strive want

WORD CULTURE
The expression *less is more* means that simplicity is better than embellishment. The phrase is associated with architect Ludwig Mies van der Rohe, who thought it best to keep visual clutter in buildings to a minimum.

*We live in a society continuously **striving** for more.*

The more we have, the happier we are—or so we tell ourselves.

Now, there's a well-known saying that "less is more," but is this always true? That's what we'll determine in this unit as we examine the issues of voluntary simplicity (anti-consumerism) and caloric restriction.

SECTION A
Voluntary Simplicity

Examines the anti-consumerism lifestyle.

SECTION B
Caloric Restriction

Examines the effects of a low-calorie, high-nutrient diet.

Voluntary Simplicity

Did You Know?

adherent partisan

espouse promote

enlightenment illumination

Voluntary simplicity is an anti-consumerist lifestyle whose **adherents** keep personal consumption to a strict minimum. They voluntarily choose to lead simpler lives for spiritual, political and health reasons. Indeed, many of the world's great religions **espouse** voluntary simplicity as a means of attaining **enlightenment**, several political parties endorse anti-consumerism as a method of protecting the environment and a growing number of people embrace simple living as a way of reducing work-related stress in their lives.

Most who live simply are concerned about reducing their carbon footprint (the amount of carbon dioxide emitted as a result of daily activities). Tools to reduce one's carbon footprint include:
- telecommuting (using the Internet to work from home)
- eating locally grown foods
- avoiding advertising, especially on TV, to reduce the temptation to overconsume

While voluntary simplicity may not be for everyone, it seems to work out well for some. On the next page are arguments for both sides of the issue.

Adopting a simple-living lifestyle is right because it:	Adopting a simple-living lifestyle is wrong because it:
1. helps the environment.	1. harms the economy.
2. allows one to live more fully.	2. deprives one of life's pleasures.

What's the Buzz?

Let's personalize the issue of voluntary simplicity.

spare time free time

goal objective

- For each of the five statements below, indicate whether you strongly disagree, disagree, neither agree nor disagree, agree or strongly agree.
- Be prepared to discuss your answers with the class.

Statement	Strongly disagree	Disagree	Neither agree nor disagree	Agree	Strongly agree
1. Having **spare time** is more important than earning money.	☐	☐	☐	☐	☐
2. Having a job that pays very well is one of my **goals**.	☐	☐	☐	☐	☐
3. I would prefer not to own a car.	☐	☐	☐	☐	☐
4. I would be unhappy without my possessions.	☐	☐	☐	☐	☐
5. It is important to live within walking distance of where I work (or study).	☐	☐	☐	☐	☐

Discussion

- Get into small groups.
- Consider the questions at the top of page 84.
- Present your findings to the rest of the class.

Note: As one group makes its presentation, your teacher may intervene and ask you for *your* opinion. Be prepared.

1. Why do you buy things? List at least three different reasons.

2. How do you feel when you buy something new?

3. Do you ever buy things you do not need and cannot afford? Explain.

Have You Read?

For additional reading practice, visit the companion website.

Susan Semanak's article "Living Your Life without Worry" appeared in Victoria's *Times Colonist* on August 22, 2005. The article focuses on Didier DiCamillo, a Montreal translator who has chosen to live the simple life.

Before Reading

- Study the defined words and comprehension questions before reading the article—skim the text for the main ideas and scan for answers to the questions.

Now, where can I put this?

While Reading

When reading articles in your first language, do you ever encounter a word you don't know? The answer is probably "yes." While you may look the word up in a dictionary, most people can guess the meaning from the context in which the word is used. Apply this strategy to English as well. Without using a dictionary, try to guess the meaning of the word *motley* from the context in which it is used (line 36).

BY SUSAN SEMANAK

freelance self-employed

aim objective

Brown-bag lunches and clipped coupons have always been a way of life for Didier DiCamillo. He's a **freelance** translator whose **aim** is to work part-time to earn just enough to support a modest lifestyle that includes travel, volunteer work and time to read.

5   DiCamillo sold his car last year, so now he rides his bike and takes the subway. The books he reads come mostly from the library and his Internet provider is a café where he takes advantage of free wi-fi. He buys his clothes on sale and doesn't watch TV commercials to avoid the tempta-

stuff things

tion to buy **stuff**.

10   In a culture in which where you live, what you drive and how much you earn define who you are, DiCamillo is a paradox. But now trend watchers and sociologists have given a name to DiCamillo's determination to **pare**

pare down reduce

down: voluntary simplicity.

It's also known as sustainable living or simple living.

15   It's a response, they say, to the rampant consumerism of the 1980s and '90s that put so many North American families deep in debt as they juggled car loans and mortgages, credit-card bills and lines of credit.

But it's not just about money. We're time-crunched, too, clocking longer hours at work, chauffeuring the children to activities, filling our "leisure"

20   time with organized activities like classes, outings and excursions.

"People used to talk about relationships and ideas, but now it seems all we ever talk about is our stuff, or about how busy we are, how little time we have," DiCamillo lamented.

Simple living is about living deliberately, writes Janet Luhrs, author of the

25   best-selling *Simple Living Guide* (Broadway Books). "It's about being fully

aware conscious

aware of why you are living your life, and knowing that life is one you have chosen thoughtfully.

"You choose your existence rather than sailing through life on automatic pilot."

30   But living simply isn't necessarily easy.

For those who wish they could, there are university courses and grass-

guidance counsel

roots groups to offer **guidance**.

In Montreal, there's a new group DiCamillo co-founded last spring called Montreal Simple Living, whose members meet twice a month to share

35   ideas and philosophies.

lawyer legal
representative

The meetings attract a motley group—an overworked **lawyer**, a struggling economist-turned-poet who's just published her first book of haiku, a student who wheels in on his bike, carrot juice in hand, and a sixty-something woman who worries she works too much.

set up establish

proponent supporter

spend time with be with

40 The Canadian guru of the simple-living movement is author Mark Burch, who teaches a course on the subject at the University of Winnipeg and has just **set up** a resource centre dedicated to simplicity.

Proponents gravitate toward simple living for varying reasons. Some have suffered health and relationship breakdowns as a result of overwork
45 and indebtedness. Others, many of them young people, embrace it with a sense of environmental stewardship, "because they want to live lightly on the Earth," Burch said.

"Research has shown, over numerous studies, that people are happiest when engaged in work and relationships that matter to them," he said.

50 Burch says simple living is not something to be embarked upon like a New Year's resolution. It takes commitment and introspection, and is most successfully introduced incrementally.

Start by taking public transit, he suggests. Don't go to the mall unless you need something. Eliminate the credit-card balance and the line of credit.
55 Minimize social engagements with people you hardly know, but **spend** more intimate **time with** friends and family.

565 words

Reading Comprehension

▬ Respond to each of the questions.

1. List two ways in which Didier DiCamillo saves money on food.

    a) _____

    b) _____

2. List three things that Didier DiCamillo likes to do.

    a) _____

    b) _____

    c) _____

3. Circle the correct answer(s). More than one response is possible. Didier DiCamillo:
    a) takes public transit.
    b) borrows the books he reads.
    c) uses free Internet.
    d) buys used clothing.
    e) avoids watching TV commercials.

4. A *paradox* is a contradiction. Why is Didier DiCamillo a paradox?

    _____

    _____

    _____

5. List two other terms for voluntary simplicity.

a) _____ **b)** _____

6. List four types of debt mentioned in the text.

a) _____ **c)** _____

b) _____ **d)** _____

7. Voluntary simplicity is about having fewer debts and more time to do the things that really matter. TRUE ☐ FALSE ☐

8. Many older people adopt a simple living lifestyle because of health and relationship problems resulting from overwork and debt. Why do many younger people adopt a simple living lifestyle?

_____

_____

9. What advice does Mark Burch give to those wanting to adopt a simple-living lifestyle? List four pieces of advice.

a) _____

b) _____

c) _____

d) _____

10. What is the main idea of this article?
   a) Everyone should adopt a simple-living lifestyle.
   b) A simple-living lifestyle is environmentally unfriendly.
   c) Simple living is a lifestyle adopted by a diversity of people.
   d) Simple living is about having nothing.

Additional question: Were you able to determine the meaning of the word *motley* from the context alone?

Reading Discussion

■ In small groups, discuss your answers to each of the questions below.

■ Be prepared to share your group's ideas with the rest of the class.

1. Do you agree with simple-life proponents who claim that having fewer possessions makes life more enjoyable? Why or why not?

shelter place to live

2. If you could only keep one possession other than food, clothing and **shelter**, what would it be? Explain your choice.

3. With ownership comes responsibility. List two responsibilities associated with owning each of the following:
   a) a car
   b) a cellphone
   c) a very expensive piece of jewellery
   Note: Do not mention the same responsibility twice.

Word Work

In the previous section, ten terms were defined for you.

Adjectives	Expression	Nouns	Verbs
1. aware 2. freelance	3. spend time with	4. ~~aim~~ 5. guidance 6. lawyer 7. proponent 8. stuff	9. pare down 10. set up

- In the text below, there are ten terms in italics. Replace each of the terms with one of the terms from the list above.
- Pluralize nouns as required. The first one has been done for you as an example.

I confess. I am a "shopaholic." My *objective* (1. _____aim_____) in life is to buy *things* (2. _____)—clothes, china, furniture—you name it, I buy it!

I came to this obsession honestly: my mother, a *legal representative* (3. _____), and my father, a *self-employed* (4. _____) journalist, made enough money when I was growing up to buy whatever they wanted. Unfortunately, they were always too busy earning money to *be with* (5. _____) me, so they bought me things to compensate. I got so used to getting things, that I simply continued the "getting" on my own when I left home in my early twenties.

As the years passed, I never really gave my "shopaholism" much thought—until the other day, that is. I had just received some new acquisitions—a new winter coat (my fourteenth!), a set of china and a sofa—when I realized that I had nowhere to put the items: I either had to rent a storage locker or *reduce* (6. _____) my possessions.

So what did I do? I rented a storage locker, of course!

While signing the rental agreement, I was painfully *conscious* (7. _____) that my buying problem was indeed out of control: I urgently needed some *counsel* (8. _____), so I went straight out and bought a few books on simple living! (Yes, I know how ironic this is!) Inspired by what I had read, I *established* (9. _____) a simple-living club composed of several simple-living *supporters* (10. _____) like myself.

While I have a long way to go before I divest myself of all my worldly possessions, I have made some progress: I sold off all the stuff in my storage locker! And you know what? I haven't missed any of those things one little bit!

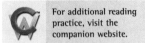

Have You Heard?

For additional reading practice, visit the companion website.

Anne Lagacé Dowson hosts the CBC call-in show *Radio Noon*, broadcast out of Montreal. On May 25, 2007, Ms. Wood spoke with guest Issa (formerly known as Jane Siberry, a well-known Canadian singer) about voluntary simplicity.

Pre-listening Vocabulary

- Match each word with its definition. The first one has been done for you as an example.
- After verifying your answers with your teacher, find a partner. On a separate sheet of paper, correctly use the ten terms in ten sentences of your own. Each partner is responsible for writing five sentences that demonstrate the correct usage of the terms.

Terms	Definitions
1. couch (n.) _____h_____	a) scenery or panorama
2. divest oneself of something (exp.) _____	b) an announcement
3. jewellery (n.) _____	c) take control

Terms	Definitions
4. landscape (n.) _____	d) merchandise
5. material goods (exp.) _____	e) ask oneself
6. notice (n.) _____	f) value highly
7. roots (n.) _____	g) give something away
8. take over (v.) _____	h) sofa
9. treasure (v.) _____	i) cultural or family origins
10. wonder (v.) _____	j) ornaments for the body, such as rings, necklaces, bracelets, etc.

LISTENING STRATEGY
Where are the "best seats" in a classroom? In the front, of course! Why? Because there are fewer distractions. Effective listeners are focused listeners.

While Listening

You will listen to the interview twice.

- The first time, listen for the general idea.
- The second time, listen for the details, taking point-form notes to help you remember the information.

Listening Comprehension

- Referring to your notes, respond to each of the questions.

1. Why did Issa have difficulty getting to the studio?

_____

_____

_____

2. Issa's decision to adopt a simple-living lifestyle was impulsive.   TRUE ☐ FALSE ☐

3. What was Issa looking at when she made the decision to sell her house and adopt a simple-living lifestyle?

_____

_____

4. How long did it take for Issa's house to sell?

_____

5. Fill in the blank. "I put effort into it, and the universe made it happen at the right time for me 'cause it's quite hard to do. And I don't think one is meant to rip your _____ out too quickly, but it was the right time for me." (Issa)

6. Circle the letter(s) of the correct answer(s). More than one response is possible. Issa:
   a) sent an email out to people who might want to buy her possessions.
   b) had a house-contents sale.
   c) sold couches, beds, paintings, dishes, artwork, dresses, jewellery, stage clothes, etc.
   d) sold her Manolo Blahnik[1] pumps (shoes).

7. Describe Issa's cabin in northern Ontario?

   _____

   _____

8. According to Issa, what does living in her cabin teach her?

   _____

   _____

9. Fill in the blanks. "Earlier in the program, we played one of her best- or better-known songs, 'Calling all Angels'. We're talking about voluntary simplicity, an idea that Issa ... has taken very seriously as you have just heard. She's basically divested herself of most of her _____ _____ ...."

10. Choose the letter of the correct answer. The interview is about:
    a) the need for everyone to adopt a simple-living lifestyle.
    b) one woman's journey toward living more simply.
    c) a Canadian singer who changed her name.
    d) how to live more simply.

    _____
    1. Famous Spanish designer

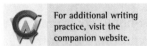

Would You Write That Down?

Your teacher may ask you to complete one or both of the writing activities below. If asked to write an essay, be sure to structure your writing clearly.

Free-form Writing

■ Write a 50- to 65-word paragraph in response to one of the following questions:

1. Would you be able to give up watching TV (to avoid advertising)? Why or why not?

2. Describe your ideal job. Indicate the type of work and working conditions.

3. What's more important: family or career? Explain your choice.

Essay Writing

- Write a 200- to 250-word essay on one of the thesis statements below. Your teacher may assign a thesis statement (and position) or allow you to select your own.

- Do some research on the Internet to find evidence that supports your thesis statement. (See Appendix A on pages 178–187 to review the structure of a persuasive essay.)

1. Public transportation should (or should not) be free.

carbon tax pollution tax

2. A **carbon tax** is (or is not) a good idea.

3. People should (or should not) only buy their food locally.

4. Owning a car gives (does not give) one freedom.

5. Personal inheritance should (or should not) be abolished.

Would You Speak Up?

Your teacher may ask you to participate in one or more of the following speaking activities.

Discussion

- In small groups, consider one (or more) of the following questions.
- Be prepared to share your thoughts with other groups in the class.

1. A *commune* is a community in which possessions are shared. Would you be able to live in a commune? Why or why not?

2. Why is voluntary simplicity a phenomenon of the middle and upper classes?

3. Is telecommuting a lifestyle you would enjoy? Explain.

4. Which of the following would be hardest for you to live without: a cellphone, an iPod or a television? Justify your choice.

5. With music downloading, CDs are no longer necessary. Should governments prohibit the sale of CDs to reduce the music industry's carbon footprint?

Discourse

- Prepare a structured, three-minute speech on one of the thesis statements at the top of page 93. (See Appendix B on pages 188–190 for a suggested speech structure.)

- Do some research to find evidence that supports your chosen thesis statement.
  Make sure your speech has an introduction, a development and a conclusion.

1. People should (or should not) pay for tap water.

2. Watching TV encourages (or does not encourage) overconsumption.

3. Society should (or should not) prohibit the sale of newspapers.

4. The government should (or should not) tax bicycles.

5. The sale of gasoline-powered cars should (or should not) be prohibited.

Debate

■ Debate the following proposal: Adopting a simple-living lifestyle is wrong. (See Appendix B on pages 190–193 for the rules of debate.)

What's That Word Mean Again?

In the reading and listening sections, we focused on twenty terms—ten from each section. The activity below is designed to help you review some of this vocabulary.

Vocabulary Activity: Hangman

The game "hangman" is a fun and easy way to revise vocabulary. If you've got a couple of minutes, why not find a partner and play a few games?

Required
• Pen or pencil
• Five sheets of blank paper
• A bit of luck!

Procedure
1. With a partner, review the twenty terms presented in the reading and listening sections of this part of Unit 4.

2. Set up a hangman game as indicated in the illustration on page 94.

3. Partner A secretly chooses a word form the list and draws a series of dashes, one for each letter in the word.

4. Partner B guesses a letter. If Partner B guesses correctly, Partner A writes the letter on the appropriate dash. If Partner B guesses incorrectly, Partner A draws part of the hanged man's body.

5. A point is awarded when Partner B guesses the word **or** when Partner A completes the drawing of the hanged man before the word is guessed.

6. Start a new game, changing roles.

7. Play "best three out of five."

Do not look at the word list while you are actually playing the game.

Suggestion: The drawing of the hanged man is considered complete when there is a body (including a trunk, two arms and two legs) and a heart! (In other words, six letter guesses are allowed.)

Would You Like to Work Together?

In this section, you are asked to work with another student on a speaking project.

Project Overview

spending exchanging money for goods and services

You and your partner are going to interview each other about your **spending** habits. Before the interview, you must construct a list of relevant questions.

Instructions

1. Working together, write down twenty questions about spending on a single sheet of paper. Number your questions.

2. Submit your questions to your teacher for correction.

3. Rewrite your corrected questions on twenty small slips of paper—one question per slip.

4. Place the slips of paper in a container (hat, envelope, etc.)

5. Taking turns, select slips of paper and read the questions to your partner.

point form listing of main ideas in one or two words, not using complete sentences

6. Write down your partner's responses in **point form**.

7. Continue asking and answering questions until all twenty slips of paper have been selected.

8. Review your partner's answers and select two or three points of interest; present these points to the class. (The more interesting your questions, the more interesting your presentation will be!)

Your teacher may (or may not) evaluate your question formation and content.

Caloric Restriction

Did You Know?

aging getting old

Caloric restriction (CR) is the practice of limiting the number of calories consumed to improve health and slow down the **aging** process.

weight mass

Those who practise a CR lifestyle:
- maintain body **weights** below recommended norms;
- consume fewer than the recommended number of calories on a daily basis;
- optimize the nutritional content of the foods they eat.

In this way, CR goes beyond dieting—the goal of which is to *temporarily* reduce caloric consumption to attain a normal weight. CR is, as one expert claims, "dieting plus."

While CR research conducted on animal and human subjects is promising, CR is not without its critics who maintain that a diet low in calories may damage muscle tissue and may not provide subjects with enough calories to permit regular exercise—an activity which also increases longevity and improves health.

forgo abstain from

So the question is this: Would you be willing to **forgo** your favourite foods to keep the Grim Reaper away? (Or would you prefer to indulge—and take your chances with Mr. Reaper?) This is one of the many questions you'll be asked to consider in this unit.

WORD CULTURE
The *Grim Reaper*, a fictional character, refers to death. This name is a combination of the expression *grim death* and the artistic depiction of death as a figure carrying a scythe, a tool used to cut grass.

Adopting a caloric restriction lifestyle is **right** because it:	Adopting a caloric restriction lifestyle is **wrong** because it:
1. promotes health.	1. diminishes quality of life.
2. reduces consumption.	2. is an unsustainable lifestyle.

What's the Buzz?

Let's personalize the issue of caloric restriction.

- For each of the five statements below, indicate whether you strongly disagree, disagree, neither agree nor disagree, agree or strongly agree.
- Be prepared to discuss your answers with the class.

Statement	Strongly disagree	Disagree	Neither agree nor disagree	Agree	Strongly agree
1. Junk food tastes great.	☐	☐	☐	☐	☐
2. Eating is one of life's greatest pleasures.	☐	☐	☐	☐	☐
3. **Fasting** is healthy.	☐	☐	☐	☐	☐
4. It is difficult not to **overeat** in North American society.	☐	☐	☐	☐	☐
5. **Processed foods** are unhealthy.	☐	☐	☐	☐	☐

fasting going without food

overeat eat too much

processed foods natural foods transformed and sold by companies

Discussion

- Get into small groups.
- Consider the questions below.
- Present your findings to the rest of the class.

Note: As one group makes its presentation, your teacher may intervene and ask you for *your* opinion. Be prepared.

1. What constitutes a healthy diet?

2. Would you like to live to be more than 100? Why or why not?

give up stop using or doing something

3. Could you **give up** junk food entirely? Explain.

Jim Salter is an Associated Press writer whose article "Pass the Celery" appeared in the *Hamilton Spectator* on January 14, 2006.

Before Reading

■ Read the defined words and comprehension questions before reading the article— skim the text for the main ideas and scan for answers to the questions.

READING STRATEGY

Some people find it helpful to "read with their hands," meaning they underline, highlight and annotate texts as they read.

While Reading

WORD CULTURE

The expression *ripe old age* means "very old." The expression itself is of a ripe old age, dating back to the sixteenth century.

When reading articles in your first language, do you ever encounter a word you don't know? The answer is probably "yes." While you may look the word up in a dictionary, most people can guess the meaning from the context in which the word is used. Apply this strategy to English as well. Without using a dictionary, try to guess the meaning of the expression *on average* from the context in which it is used (line 10).

VOCABULARY TIP

Don't confuse the word *researcher* with *searcher*. A *researcher* is a person who methodically studies something: Researchers will find a cure for cancer. A *searcher* is a person who looks for something or someone: The searchers found the lost child.

PASS THE CELERY:
I'M SEVENTY BUT MY HEART'S ONLY FIFTY-FIVE

BY JIM SALTER
HAMILTON SPECTATOR

study scientific
investigation

An extremely low-calorie diet helps the heart age more slowly, according to researchers who released what they call the first-ever human **study** on the subject.

finding result
benefit advantage

5 The **findings** confirmed earlier studies on mice and rats that demonstrate the cardiac **benefits** of a restricted-calorie diet.

The study looked at the heart function of twenty-five members of the Caloric Restriction Society, ages forty-one to sixty-four, who consume 1,400 to 2,000 nutritionally balanced calories per day. They were compared to twenty-five people who eat a typical Western diet, consuming 2,000 to
10 3,000 daily calories on average.

intake consumption

The result: Those limiting caloric **intake** had the heart functions of much younger people—typically about fifteen years younger than their age. Ultrasound exams showed group members had hearts that appeared more elastic than most people their age; their hearts were also able to
15 relax between beats in a way similar to hearts in younger people.

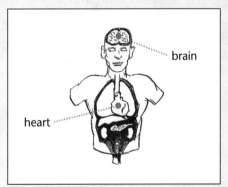

In healthy people, the heart at rest beats about 60 to 100 times a minute.

"This is the first study to demonstrate that long-term calorie restriction with optimal nutrition has cardiac-specific effects that delay (or reverse) age-associated declines in heart function," said Luigi Fontana, lead author and assistant professor of medicine at Washington University in
20 St. Louis.

The study will be published Tuesday in the *Journal of the American College of Cardiology*.

Fontana said simply consuming less food is not the answer. Members of the study group eat food resembling a traditional Mediterranean diet,
25 focusing on vegetables, olive oil, beans, whole grains, fish and fruit. They avoid refined and processed foods, soft drinks, desserts, white bread and other sources of "empty" calories.

stringent rigorous

heart attack cardiac arrest

stroke stoppage of blood flow to the brain

relative family member
unlikely improbable
genetic makeup genetic constitution

For the general public, the researchers recommend a moderate reduction in calories, combined with moderate, regular exercise.

30 Research on mice and rats indicated that lifespan can be stretched by about thirty percent with **stringent** and consistent caloric restriction. That research also suggested that restricting calories can help prevent cancer.

Heart attacks and **strokes** cause about forty percent of deaths in
35 Western countries, researchers said. Cancer causes another thirty percent.

Fontana said those deaths are attributable to "secondary aging" from high cholesterol, diabetes, high blood pressure and other often-preventable conditions.

While it has long been known that a healthy diet and exercise can reduce
40 risks, the study suggests that caloric restriction combined with optimal nutrition can do even more.

Fontana said most participants in the study had immediate **relatives** who suffered heart attacks or strokes, so it was **unlikely** their **genetic makeup** was a contributing factor to their unusually healthy hearts.

45 "We don't know how long each individual will end up living, but they certainly have a longer life expectancy than average because they're most likely not going to die from a heart attack, stroke or diabetes," said professor John Holloszy, who worked on the study.

"And if, in fact, their hearts are aging more slowly, it's conceivable they'll
50 live for a very long time."

485 words

Reading Comprehension

■ Respond to each of the questions.

1. Studies indicate that a calorie-restricted diet is beneficial to the cardiac health of humans and lab animals. TRUE ☐ FALSE ☐

2. How many calories do members of the Caloric Restriction Society consume per day? A typical Westerner?

_____

3. In your own words, what was the "first-ever" human study's main finding?

_____

_____

_____

4. Simplify the following quotation from the article by rewriting the quotation in your own words: "This is the first study to demonstrate that long-term calorie restriction with optimal nutrition has cardiac-specific effects that delay (or reverse) age-associated declines in heart function …."

_____

_____

_____

_____

5. Which of the following statements is **false**?
   a) The human study indicates that an individual need only reduce food consumption to receive cardiac benefits.
   b) Those who received cardiac benefits ate a Mediterranean diet.
   c) In general, those who received cardiac benefits ate highly nutritious foods.

6. Based on the human study's findings, what two recommendations did the researchers make for the general population?
   a) _____
   b) _____

7. What causes "secondary aging"?

_____

_____

_____

8. Why is it significant that the members of the Caloric Restriction Society who participated in the study had immediate relatives who had suffered heart attacks and strokes?

_____

_____

_____

9. Find two terms in the article which mean "expected length of life."
   a) _____   b) _____

10. Which statement best summarizes the main idea of the article?
    a) Studies show that when individuals eat less, they live longer.
    b) Studies show that individuals should adopt a Mediterranean diet.
    c) Human and animal studies suggest that eating low-calorie, high-nutrient food improves cardiac function and may increase lifespan.
    d) Individuals with slowly aging hearts live longer.

Additional question: Were you able to determine the meaning of the expression *on average* from the context alone?

Reading Discussion

- In small groups, discuss your answers to each of the questions below.
- Be prepared to share your group's ideas with the rest of the class.

1. Would you describe your current diet as healthy or unhealthy? Explain.

2. Would you be willing to adhere stringently to a Mediterranean diet to live longer? Why or why not?

3. List ten foods that contain "empty" calories.

Word Work

In the previous section, ten terms were defined for you:

Adjectives	Expressions	Nouns
1. stringent 2. unlikely	3. genetic makeup 4. ~~heart attack~~	5. benefit 6. finding 7. intake 8. relative 9. stroke 10. study

- In the following text, there are ten terms in italics. Replace each of the terms with one of the terms from the list above.
- Pluralize nouns as required. The first one has been done for you as an example.

It was love at first bite.

I still remember the time I sat down to eat my first "poutine": the crispy french fries, the fresh cheese curds and the unctuous gravy. What a delight!

I was seventeen at the time, and unconcerned about my health, for I was invincible! Until I turned forty, that is. Then, I had to reconsider both my poor diet and my lack of exercise in order to avoid the imminent *cardiac arrest* (1. _____heart attack_____) or *stoppage of blood flow to the brain* (2. _____): my *genetic constitution* (3. _____) was far from exceptional, and any of my *family members* (4. _____) who had successfully avoided the *advantages* (5. _____) of healthy living had gone to their graves early.

While it is *improbable* (6. _____) that the occasional "empty calorie" will shorten one's lifespan, a recent *scientific investigation* (7. _____) has demonstrated that a diet consisting solely of processed foods, soft drinks and desserts speeds up the aging process; for those wanting to live to a ripe old age, such a *result* (8. _____) cannot be ignored.

Now, I won't say that "eating right" is easy. It's not. While I adhere to a *rigorous* (9._____) regime most of the time—nearly eliminating my *consumption* (10._____) of fast foods—I will admit to the occasional meal of french fries covered with cheese and gravy.

I guess one never forgets one's first love.

Have You Heard?

 For additional listening practice, visit the companion website.

You will be watching two *CTV News* segments covering the findings of a human study on the effects of caloric restriction.

In the first segment you will be watching medical specialist Avis Favaro's report, which aired on April 4, 2006. Featured guests include study participant Scott Westbrook, researcher Dr. Steven Smith and dietician Rosie Schwartz. Chief anchor and senior editor Lloyd Robertson provides an introduction to the report.

In the second segment you will be watching *Canada AM* host Seamus O'Regan's interview of one of the study's researchers, Dr. Steven Smith. Mr. O'Regan's interview aired on April 5, 2006.

Pre-watching Vocabulary

▬ Match each term with its definition. The first one has been done for you as an example.

▬ After verifying your answers with your teacher, find a partner. On a separate sheet of paper, correctly use the ten terms in ten sentences of your own creation. Each partner is responsible for writing five sentences that demonstrate the correct usage of the terms.

Segment 1

Terms		Definitions
1. cell (n.)	_e_	a) abbreviation of *deoxyribonucleic acid*, a substance that carries an organism's genetic information
2. DNA (n.)	_____	b) make longer
3. lengthen (v.)	_____	c) breathe noisily while sleeping
4. snore (v.)	_____	d) damage due to usage
5. wear and tear (exp.)	_____	e) basic unit of a living organism

Segment 2

Terms		Definitions
6. adverse (adj.)	_____	f) get used to
7. become accustomed to (exp.)	_____	g) related organisms capable of interbreeding
8. be on the lookout (exp.)	_____	h) secondary medical effect
9. side effect (n.)	_____	i) watch carefully
10. species (n.)	_____	j) negative or unfavourable

While Watching

You will watch the report twice.

- The first time you watch, try to understand the general idea.
- The second time you watch, listen for the details, taking point-form notes to help you remember the information.
- Referring to your notes, respond to each of the comprehension questions.

Segment 1

1. Fill in the blanks. "This first study of its kind on humans found those who cut daily calorie intake by one quarter created conditions that could _____ their lives."

2. Study participant Scott Westbrook mentions four benefits he experienced as a result of caloric restriction. List two.

   a) _____

   b) _____

3. According to scientists, why is eating less good for the body?

_____

_____

_____

4. Which of the following statements is **false**?
   a) Caloric restriction may help prevent cancer.
   b) Most participants felt hungry during the study.
   c) Most North Americans overeat.

5. Which statement best summarizes the main idea of the report?
   a) The benefits of caloric restriction outweigh any associated risks.
   b) Further studies on caloric restriction need to be conducted; in the mean-
   time, North Americans should stop overeating.
   c) Overeating causes cancer.
   d) North Americans are overweight.

Segment 2
   6. Fill in the blanks. "Everyone's always _____ _____ _____

   for ways to slow down the aging process. Well, a new study by the *Journal*

   of the American Medical Association says that a small change in your diet

   can do just that." (O'Regan)

   7. a) How many people participated in Dr. Smith's study? _____

   b) How long did the study last? _____

   c) By what percentage did the study's participants decrease their recommended calorie intake? _____

   8. Circle the correct answer(s). More than one response is possible.
   Caloric restriction:
   a) was initially difficult for the study's participants; however, restriction
   became easier (and even enjoyable) with time.
   b) slows down the metabolism.
   c) reduces body temperature.
   d) causes hormonal changes in the body.
   e) guarantees a longer human lifespan.
   f) is no different from dieting.

   9. Some participants experienced serious side   TRUE ☐ FALSE ☐
   effects due to caloric restriction.

   10. Which statement best summarizes the main idea of the report?
   a) In order to live longer, people should adopt a caloric-restriction lifestyle.
   b) Studies on caloric restriction prove that eating fewer calories increases
   human longevity.
   c) Initial findings from a study on human caloric restriction indicate that
   caloric restriction can be beneficial to human health.
   d) It's too early for people to adopt a caloric-restriction lifestyle, as poten-
   tially negative side effects have not been thoroughly studied.

Would You Write That Down?

For additional writing practice, visit the companion website.

Your teacher may ask you to complete one or both of the writing activities below. If asked to write an essay, be sure to structure your writing clearly.

Free-form Writing

- Write a 50- to 65-word paragraph in response to one of the following questions:

1. Describe your diet.

2. Does dieting work? Explain.

3. Should people count calories? Why or why not?

Essay Writing

WRITING SUGGESTION
When submitting a written assignment, get on your teacher's good side by writing legibly and double-spacing your copy.

- Write a 200- to 250-word essay on one of the thesis statements below. Your teacher may assign a thesis statement (and position) or allow you to select your own.
- Do some research on the Internet to find evidence that supports your thesis statement. (See Appendix A on pages 178–187 to review the structure of a persuasive essay.)

1. North American society is (or is not) obsessed with food.

2. Dieting is (or is not) healthy.

3. Junk food should (or should not) be banned from school and hospital cafeterias.

4. Fast food restaurants should (or should not) label every food item sold with its nutritional content.

5. Exercise is (or is not) enjoyable.

Would You Speak Up?

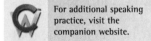

For additional speaking practice, visit the companion website.

Your teacher may ask you to participate in one or more of the following speaking activities.

Discussion

- In small groups, consider one (or more) of the following questions.
- Be prepared to share your thoughts with other groups in the class.

1. A "crash diet" is an extreme (and unhealthy) diet designed for rapid weight loss. Name one crash diet and list three potential side effects of this diet.

2. Is it possible to be overweight *and* healthy? Why or why not?

3. What's the ideal lifespan?

4. Why do people fast? Give at least two reasons.

5. Should parents control their children's diets?

Discourse

- Prepare a structured, three-minute speech on one of the thesis statements below. (See Appendix B on pages 188–190 for a suggested speech structure.)
- Do some research to find evidence that supports your chosen thesis statement.
- Make sure your speech has an introduction, a development and a conclusion.

1. Junk-food packaging should (or should not) contain warning labels.

2. Fasting is (or is not) healthy.

3. Yo-yo dieting is (or is not) harmful.

4. A nutritious diet has to (or does not have to) include meat.

5. College physical education courses should (or should not) be optional.

Debate

- Debate the following proposal: Adopting a caloric restriction lifestyle is wrong. (See Appendix B on pages 190–193 for the rules of debate.)

 What's That Word Mean Again?

In the reading and listening sections, we focused on twenty terms—ten from each section. The activity below is designed to help you review some of this vocabulary.

Vocabulary Activity: Hangman

The game "hangman" is a fun and easy way to revise vocabulary. If you've got a couple of minutes, why not find a partner and play a few games?

Required
- Pen or pencil
- Five sheets of blank paper
- A bit of luck!

Procedure

1. With a partner, review the twenty terms presented in the reading and listening sections of this part of Unit 4.

2. Set up a hangman game as indicated in the illustration.

3. Partner A secretly chooses a word form the list and draws a series of dashes, one for each letter in the word.

4. Partner B guesses a letter. If Partner B guesses correctly, Partner A writes the letter on the appropriate dash. If Partner B guesses incorrectly, Partner A draws part of the hanged man's body.

5. A point is awarded when Partner B guesses the word **or** when Partner A completes the drawing of the hanged man before the word is guessed.

6. Start a new game, changing roles.

7. Play "best three out of five."

Do not look at the word list while you are actually playing the game.

Suggestion: The drawing of the hanged man is considered complete when there is a body (including a trunk, two arms and two legs) and a heart! (In other words, six letter guesses are allowed.)

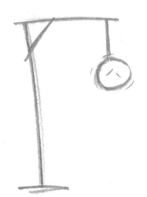

Would You Like to Work Together?

In this section, you are asked to work with another student on a speaking project.

Project Overview

You and your partner are going to interview each other about your food habits. Before the interview, you must construct a list of relevant questions.

Instructions

1. Working together, write down twenty questions about food habits on a single sheet of paper. Number your questions.

2. Submit your questions to your teacher for correction.

3. Rewrite your corrected questions on twenty small slips of paper—one question per slip.

point form listing of main ideas in one or two words, not using complete sentences

4. Place the slips of paper in a container (hat, envelope, etc.)

5. Taking turns, select slips of paper and read the questions to your partner.

6. Write down your partner's responses in **point form**.

7. Continue asking and answering questions until all twenty slips of paper have been selected.

8. Review your partner's answers and select two or three points of interest; present these points to the class. (The more interesting your questions, the more interesting your presentation will be!)

Your teacher may (or may not) evaluate your question formation and content.

UNIT 5 — Are We Prisoners of Our Cells?

The title of this unit refers to the cellphones that we use to communicate with one another as well as the cells that constitute the basic units of our bodies. The title is also a **pun** in that a "cell" is a room in which prisoners are held.

pun play on words

Are we prisoners of our cellphones?

Are we prisoners of our biology?

These are just two of the fundamental questions we will consider in Unit 5.

When they reengineer him, maybe they can make him smarter!

SECTION A

Restricting Juvenile Cellphone Usage

Examines the issue of restricting young people's rights and privileges.

SECTION B

Eugenics

Examines the issue of "perfecting" the human species.

Restricting Juvenile Cellphone Usage

Did You Know?

youth young people

purchase buy

Adults impose restrictions on **youth** that they do not impose on themselves:
- The legal minimum drinking age for Canadians is eighteen or nineteen, depending on the province or territory;
- The legal minimum age to **purchase** tobacco in Canada is eighteen or nineteen, depending on the province or territory;
- The legal minimum driving age is sixteen.

And the list goes on!

Adults restrict juvenile rights to protect juveniles from themselves.

What do you think about that?

Do young people need to be protected from themselves? Are they too immature to understand the dangers of drinking? Of smoking? Are they unable to drive responsibly? Many adults would answer "yes" to these questions, and some

VOCABULARY TIP
In this unit, *juvenile* is used in the sense of "relating to young people." But this adjective can also mean "immature."

WORD CULTURE
The expression *cut someone some slack* means "give him or her a chance." The expression dates back to the mid-1900s and alludes to slackening a rope or a sail on a boat.

would even like to extend the current restrictions placed on youth to include cellphone usage. Should society increase the number of restrictions placed on young people? Or should society *cut them some slack*? This is what you will decide in this unit.

Restricting juvenile cellphone usage is right because restrictions	**Restricting juvenile cellphone usage is wrong because restrictions**
1. teach responsibility.	1. are discriminatory.
2. protect society.	2. are unenforceable.

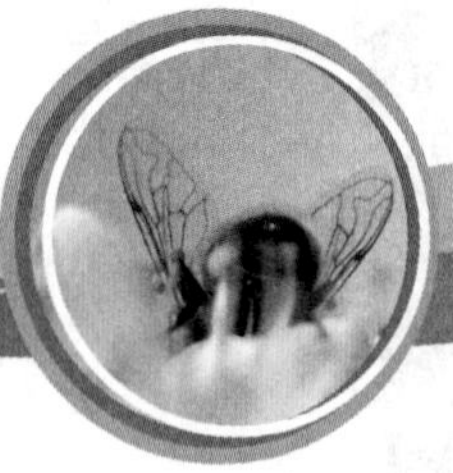

What's the Buzz?

By definition, a gadget is a small and useful—but unnecessary—device. Are you a gadget guy or gal? Find out by completing the following quiz.

worry about be concerned about

1. Your home computer is just over a year old. A new, faster and better model appears on the market. Your old computer meets your current needs. You:
a) continue using your old computer, realizing that technology is constantly evolving.
b) consider buying the new computer, but only if you can sell your old one for a decent price.
c) run out and buy the new computer—you'll **worry about** what to do with the old one later.

be fed up with (something) be tired of (something)

soaked saturated

pound place for homeless animals

2. You **are fed up with** cats and other animals coming into your backyard and ruining your gardens. A new—and extremely expensive—motion-activated sprinkler system has recently come out on the market. The moment a cat steps into your backyard, it will be **soaked**! You:
a) hold onto your money and pick up a dog at the local **pound**.
b) don't buy the expensive system, but place ordinary sprinklers in the backyard—and wait to turn them on the moment you see a cat!
c) order the system immediately—even if it means you'll have to borrow money from the bank.

pet animal kept at home

3. You have two dogs. You love your **pets**, but are fed up with constantly having to fill up their water bowl. A new pet drinking fountain is available: each time your dogs drink, the bowl automatically fills itself. You:
a) get the dogs a bigger water bowl.
b) make your own automated bowl.
c) buy the auto-filling water bowl without a moment's hesitation.

4. You buy a new eight-gigabyte (GB) iPod and excitedly call your best friend to tell him about your new purchase. Your friend congratulates you on the new iPod and casually mentions that a new 80 GB model just became available on the market. You:
   a) are pleased with your new purchase; 8 GB meets your needs.
   b) are pleased with your new purchase—but plan on upgrading in a couple of years.
   c) return to the store and exchange your 8 GB model for a more expensive 80 GB model.

5. You're always losing your keys. You learn about a remote-control key-chain finder: you press a button on a remote control unit, and the key chain starts to beep! No more lost keys! You:
   a) put up a hook just inside your front door and hang your keys up when you come home.
   b) have an extra set of keys made.
   c) buy the remote-control key-chain finder and practise "finding" your keys.

Scoring: If most of your answers are *a* you're definitely not a gadget person. If most of your answers are *b* you like gadgets—but you like your money more! If most of your answers are *c* not only do you like gadgets, but you should probably try inventing a few because you'll need the extra income to pay for all of those gadgets!

Discussion

- Get into small groups.
- Consider the questions below.
- Present your findings to the rest of the class.

Note: As one group makes its presentation, your teacher may intervene and ask you for *your* viewpoint. Be prepared.

1. In your opinion, are the following items necessary or unnecessary? Justify your answers.
   a) cellphones
   b) PSPs[1]
   c) iPods

2. How many of the items in the previous question do you personally own? Which one is most important to you? Why?

3. Using a cellphone can be distracting, depending on the context in which it is used. Describe three contexts in which using a cellphone is unacceptably distracting.

---

1. PlayStation Portable

Have You Read?

For additional reading practice, visit the companion website.

Siobhan Bradley is a student living in Ontario. Her column appeared in the *Toronto Star* on April 19, 2007. Miss Bradley's column proves that one is never too young to explore important social issues—and take a public stand!

Before Reading

■ Read the defined words and comprehension questions before reading the article— skim the text for the main ideas and scan for answers to the questions.

READING STRATEGY
When you read, read actively. Examples of active reading include making lists and charting information. In the article you're about to read, the author enumerates several arguments to prove her point. Making a separate list of her arguments as you read would be an excellent exercise.

Yours too, Mr. Krabappel!

While Reading

VOCABULARY TIP
When looking up a word in the dictionary, don't just select the first definition you see. Many words have multiple definitions; the meaning changes according to the context in which the word is used.

Informal English differs from formal English.

    Informal English: Are you ready to *chow down*?
    Formal English: Are you ready to eat?

In the article you are about to read, two informal terms are underlined. For each of the underlined terms, come up with an equivalent term in formal English. You may wish to consult a thesauraus (a book of synonyms) or a dictionary.

DO PHONES HAVE A ROLE IN SCHOOL?

BY SIOBHAN BRADLEY

tote carry

Most teens today have some sort of mobile electronic device that they **tote** everywhere, claiming they couldn't live without this treasured possession. It could be an iPod, a PSP or an MP3 player, but cellphones are the most popular. Lots of schools have a "no electronics" policy, but that
5   definitely doesn't stop kids from bringing electronics to school.

Students can easily flip open their phones to access the Internet in order to cheat on a test while their teacher's back is turned. What is stopping someone from filming a student **brawl** or a teacher's **tantrum** and posting the outburst on the Web?

brawl fight
tantrum fit of temper

10   A cellphone is also a constant distraction from learning, because a cellphone can be used to play games, text friends, watch TV, take pictures or even take calls during class! This is why a cellphone ban is being proposed in schools that don't already have one.

prevent stop

There are some arguments that can **prevent** this ban from being issued,
15   as cellphones shouldn't always be portrayed as negative influences.

"Girls our age need cellphones in case they need to call parents or someone important but they're too embarrassed about the situation to use the office phone," says an anonymous grade-seven student at Mother Teresa Catholic School in Ajax.

20   In high schools especially, students often use their cellphones to call or text a friend to find out where their friends are at lunchtime. (You don't want to search your school from top to bottom to find someone, do you?) Or students use them to remind one another of an after-school sports practice or club meeting.

come in handy be useful

25   Also, if students want to catch up on unfinished homework during lunch, free periods or recesses, cellphones **come in handy**. Research can be completed with Internet access, and these gadgets include calculators that help with math and sometimes even dictionaries that can be used for language study. Friends can also be contacted via text messaging or phone
30   calls if someone needs homework help.

"It is ridiculous that we can't bring cellphones to school," argues a seventh-grader. "If we can't have cellphones at school that are turned off and hidden, then teachers shouldn't be allowed to have them either! I've seen tons of teachers telling us we can't bring cellphones and then they
35   pull their own cellphones out to check their messages ten minutes later."

backpack bag worn on the back
emergency crisis

"They should just be kept in **backpacks** for **emergencies**," says another anonymous grade-seven student.

Some parents also reject this proposed ban. They buy students a cell specifically for school emergencies, so they can call their child for information.

forbid not allow

40   Although my school already **forbids** electronics, I think they should be permitted during recess, lunch and after school, providing they're kept away during class and video-taking is not allowed.

staff employees

interfere obstruct

Also, teachers and **staff** shouldn't be responsible for phones that are lost or stolen because the owner should keep them safely at all times.
45 Cellphones don't need to **interfere** with the learning aspect of school; if they appear during class, the teacher should be able to take the cell away and ban electronics for a particular student, so that others who don't abuse the rules and regulations are not punished for another person's actions.

50 So what will be decided in the end? Are cellphones learning hazards, or are they tools for safety? No matter what is decided, both parents and students will be dissatisfied.

If they are forbidden, at least you can use them as much as you want out of school and you can protest when you see teachers flip open their own
55 cellphones! They're supposed to be the role models, after all, aren't they?

605 words

Reading Comprehension

■ Respond to each of the questions.

1. The "no electronics" policy in force in many schools prevents all students from bringing iPods, PSPs, MP3s and cellphones to class.   TRUE ☐ FALSE ☐

2. Circle the letter(s) of the correct answer(s). More than one response is possible. Examples of negative cellphone usage by students during class time include:
   a) cheating.
   b) filming poor behaviour.
   c) playing games.
   d) texting friends.
   e) watching TV.
   f) taking pictures.
   g) making phone calls .

3. Many schools have banned cellphones and other schools are considering a ban because cellphones distract students from learning.   TRUE ☐ FALSE ☐

4. The author believes that a cellphone ban is inevitable.   TRUE ☐ FALSE ☐

5. Circle the letter(s) of the correct answer(s). More than one response is possible. Examples of positive cellphone usage by students include:
   a) contacting parents (or guardians) about private matters.
   b) locating friends at lunch.
   c) reminding friends of extracurricular activities.
   d) researching homework assignments.
   e) helping friends with homework assignments.

6. The cellphone ban applies to students and teachers. TRUE ☐ FALSE ☐

7. Why are some parents against a cellphone ban in schools?

_____

_____

...r's school forbids cellphone usage. TRUE ☐ FALSE ☐

...or believes that an agreement can be
...n cellphone usage that will satisfy both
...d students alike. TRUE ☐ FALSE ☐

...tement best summarizes the author's thesis?
...ones should not be banned from schools.
...ones should be allowed in school, but students should not be
...:d to use their phones during class time.
...iones should be banned from schools.
...ts should decide whether cellphones ought to be banned from
...l.

)iscussion

...oups, discuss your answers to each of the questions below.
...:d to share your group's ideas with the rest of the class.

...cellphone ban in primary school apply to teachers and students
...plain your answer.

...a context in which a teacher should be allowed to confiscate a
...cellphone.

...:ellphones be banned from primary schools? High schools? Colleges?
...ties? Justify your answers.

Word Work

In the previous section, ten terms were defined for you:

Expression	Nouns	Verbs
1. come in handy	2. backpack	7. forbid
	3. brawl	8. interfere
	4. ~~emergency~~	9. prevent
	5. staff	10. tote
	6. tantrum	

- Reread the definitions provided for these terms. Then reread the sentences in which they are used to ensure that you understand how each term is used in context.

Fill in the blanks using the preceding terms. Remember to conjugate the verbs as required. The first one has been done for you as an example.

1. Calm down! It's not an _____emergency_____!

2. Have you ever heard the expression "the terrible twos"? This expression refers to two-year-old children who have a tendency to throw a _____ whenever they don't get their way.

3. I prefer to carry my books to class in a _____ rather than in a briefcase; it's easier on the arms!

4. I saw a terrible _____ last night. Two men, obviously quite drunk, started punching each other. When one of the men pulled out a knife, I called 9-1-1.

5. Is it really possible to _____ students from bringing cellphones to school?

6. My two-year-old cousin is never without her teddy bear; she _____ it with her everywhere she goes.

7. Parents should not _____ with their child's development.

8. School policy _____ students from bringing cellphones to final exams.

9. Some people think that cellphones are an unnecessary expense; however, cellphones certainly _____ _____ _____ in an emergency!

10. The company is not doing very well: many of the _____ were laid off last week. It will be hard for them to find new jobs.

Have You Heard?

Rosemary Thompson is a well-known Canadian journalist who earned her journalism degree from Carleton University in Ottawa. In 2006 and 2007, Ms. Thompson shot two short *CTV News* segments on teen drivers and cellphone usage.

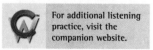

For additional listening practice, visit the companion website.

Pre-watching Vocabulary

▬ For each segment, match each word with its definition. The first one has been done for you as an example.

Segment 1

Terms		Definitions
1. brake (v.)	_e_	a) driving while intoxicated
2. drinking and driving (exp.)	_____	b) automobile device that makes noise
3. growing evidence (exp.)	_____	c) security device
4. horn (n.)	_____	d) more and more proof
5. seat belt (n.)	_____	e) slow down

Segment 2

Terms		Definitions
6. be behind the wheel (exp.)	_____	f) rule applied to some, but not all
7. dial (v.)	_____	g) be driving
8. double standard (exp.)	_____	h) drive a vehicle to the side of the road and stop
9. pull over (v.)	_____	i) observer
10. witness (n.)	_____	j) call a number on the telephone

While Watching

You will watch each segment twice.

- The first time, listen for the general idea.
- The second time, listen for the details, taking point-form notes to help you remember the information.

Watching Comprehension

- Referring to your notes, respond to each of the questions.

Segment 1

1. In your own words, explain why seventeen-year-old Laura Griffin can't listen to music when she drives.

   _____

   _____

2. Teenagers haven't gotten the message that drinking and driving is a problem.   TRUE ☐ FALSE ☐

3. Fill in the blanks. "So far only _____ and _____ has banned cellphone use while driving. This despite _____ _____ in the United States and Canada that wireless technology in cars is a major factor in accidents."[2]

4. Which of the following statements is **false**?
   a) Five high school students died in a car crash in Meaford, Ontario.
   b) The teenagers in the Meaford car crash had been drinking.
   c) Three of the teenagers in the Meaford car crash were not wearing seat belts.
   d) Investigators of the Meaford car crash are trying to discover whether distractions played a role.

5. Circle the letter of the best answer. In general, this segment is about:
   a) the dangers of drinking and driving.
   b) the dangers of dialling and driving.
   c) the dangers of being distracted and driving.
   d) teenagers who drive.

Segment 2

6. For sixteen-year-old Neil Richard, why is driving while using a cellphone not a problem?

   _____

   _____

---

2. Since this report was broadcast, Manitoba and Quebec have also banned hand-held cellphone use in cars.

7. Fill in the blanks. "The Canadian Automobile Association is calling on all provincial governments to restrict _____ _____ from using electronic gadgets, including BlackBerries and portable music players like iPods when they're _____ _____ _____."

8. In your own words, describe the accident that killed the eight-year-old boy in Montreal.

   _____

   _____

9. Which of the following statements is **false**?
   a) Student drivers in some provinces are not allowed to drive at night.
   b) Student drivers in some provinces are not allowed to drive on highways.
   c) Drivers on cellphones are five times as likely to miss signs or signals on the road and when they do see the signs or signals, they take five times as long to respond.
   d) In Newfoundland and Labrador, where cellphone use while driving is banned, 300 people have been convicted of using a cellphone while driving.

10. Circle the letter of the best answer. This segment is about:
   a) drivers' dangerous habits.
   b) the double standard of restricting cellphone usage for teen drivers, but not for adult drivers.
   c) a proposal by the Canadian Automobile Association to ban all electronic gadgets from motor vehicles.
   d) a proposal by the Canadian Automobile Association to restrict the use of electronic gadgets by inexperienced drivers.

Would You Write That Down?

For additional writing practice, visit the companion website.

Your teacher may ask you to complete one or both of the writing activities below. If asked to write an essay, be sure to structure your writing clearly.

Free-form Writing

▬ Write a 50- to 65-word paragraph in response to one of the following questions:

1. Do you own a cellphone? Why or why not?

2. Describe a situation in which you were annoyed by someone on a cellphone.

3. In your opinion, who buys more gadgets? Men or women?

Essay Writing

- Write a 200- to 250-word essay on one of the thesis statements below. Your teacher may assign a thesis statement (and position) or allow you to select your own.

- Do some research on the Internet to find evidence that supports your thesis statement. (See Appendix A on pages 178–187 to review the structure of a persuasive essay.)

1. Cellphones should (or should not) be banned from high schools.

2. Student cellphones that ring in class should (or should not) be confiscated.

3. Society should (or should not) raise the legal minimum drinking age to twenty-one.

4. A "no electronics" policy should (or should not) apply to teachers as well as students.

5. Teenagers should (or should not) be allowed to drive without an adult (twenty-one or older) present in the vehicle.

Would You Speak Up?

Your teacher may ask you to participate in one or more of the following speaking activities.

Discussion

- In small groups, consider one (or more) of the following questions.
- Be prepared to share your thoughts with other groups in the class.

1. In emergency situations, cellphones come in handy. In fact, cellphones can even save lives. Describe three emergency situations in which a cellphone can make the difference between life and death.

2. In the first video segment, new driver Laura Griffin does not listen to music while driving because she finds listening to music dangerously distracting. Is listening to music while driving dangerous for new drivers? Justify your answer.

3. In Ontario, new drivers get graduated licences: initially, new drivers are not allowed to drive alone, on highways or between the hours of **midnight** and five a.m. With time and driving experience, these restrictions are gradually removed. Do you agree or disagree with graduated licensing? Would you like to see graduated licensing extended to all new drivers, regardless of their province of origin?

midnight twelve a.m.

4. Who are better drivers? Teenaged girls or teenaged boys?

5. In her article, "Do Phones Have a Role in School?" Siobhan Bradley suggests that students be allowed to bring cellphones to school—but that they be allowed only to use them outside of class. Is such a suggestion **feasible**? Will students remember to turn off their cellphones before entering class?

feasible realistic

Discourse

- Prepare a structured, three-minute speech on one of the thesis statements below. (See Appendix B on pages 188–190 for a suggested speech structure.)
- Do some research to find evidence that supports your chosen thesis statement.
- Make sure your speech has an introduction, a development and a conclusion.

1. People should (or should not) be allowed to smoke while driving.

2. Governments should (or should not) raise the minimum driving age to twenty-one.

headset set of earphones

3. Using a hands free cellphone **headset** while driving is (or is not) dangerous.

4. Governments should (or should not) raise the legal minimum smoking age to twenty-one.

5. Using a cellphone regularly is (or is not) a health risk.

Debate

- Debate the following proposal: Restricting juvenile cellphone usage is wrong. (See Appendix B on pages 190–193 for the rules of debate.)

What's That Word Mean Again?

In the reading and listening sections, we focused on twenty terms—ten from each section. The activity below is designed to help you review some of this vocabulary.

Vocabulary Activity: Flash Cards

tried-and-true proved to be good

Flash cards are a **tried-and-true** method of vocabulary review.

Required
- Pen or pencil
- Twenty index cards
- A bit of time!

Instructions

1. Starting with the reading in Section A of this unit (pp. 115–116), write each of the ten terms in **bold** print on one side of an index card and the term's corresponding definition on the other side of the card.

2. Turning to the watching activity in Section A of this unit (p. 119), write each of the ten vocabulary terms on one side of an index card and the term's corresponding definition on the other side of the card.

3. Shuffle the cards and hold the pile of index cards "definition side up."

4. Read each definition and try to guess the defined word.

5. Give yourself a score out of twenty.

6. Repeat the activity until you have a perfect score!

Suggestion: Instead of reading the definitions yourself, have a partner read the definitions to you. This is a good way to practise your listening comprehension while reviewing and improving your vocabulary.

Would You Like to Work Together?

In this section, you are asked to work with another student on a project.

Project Overview

An "editorial" is an article in a publication that expresses the opinion of the editor. An "op-ed" is a signed article in a publication that expresses the opinion of a reader.[3] (As the term implies, an op-ed is normally published on the page opposite the editorial page.) For this project, you will each write an op-ed piece on the subject of teen curfews. Once each op-ed piece has been written, you will edit each other's work. Finally, you will submit your op-ed pieces to your teacher for evaluation.

Note: Use a word processor to write your op-ed pieces—and don't forget to use a spellchecker!

Writing an Op-Ed Piece

A good op-ed piece is informative, entertaining and succinct. Here are some suggestions:

1. Tell some kind of story related to the subject matter: a personal story or current event.

2. Provide general information about the subject: arguments in favour of teen curfews and arguments opposed.

3. Give your point of view on the subject: use examples to support your point of view.

4. Make a specific recommendation.

5. Include a byline, a one-sentence description of who you are: "Jane Doe is a humanities student at a Montreal-area college."

6. Title your work.

7. Whenever possible, use humour!

Pretend you are writing to a good friend whose opinion about the subject is the opposite of yours: try to convince your friend that your opinion is the right one!

Peer Editing

Peer editing is a three-step process that involves complimenting, suggesting and correcting:

1. Make compliments: story or current event, word choice, organization, use of humour, etc.

2. Make suggestions: more evocative vocabulary, shorter (or longer) sentences, improved focus, etc.

3. Make corrections: spelling, punctuation and grammar.

Submission

Retype your edited op-ed pieces, making sure to double-space and leave a 2.5 cm margin. Submit your project to your teacher.

---

3. In the reading section of Unit 5A, you read an op-ed piece by grade-seven student Siobhan Bradley, who expressed her opinion against a "no-electronics" policy at her school.

Eugenics

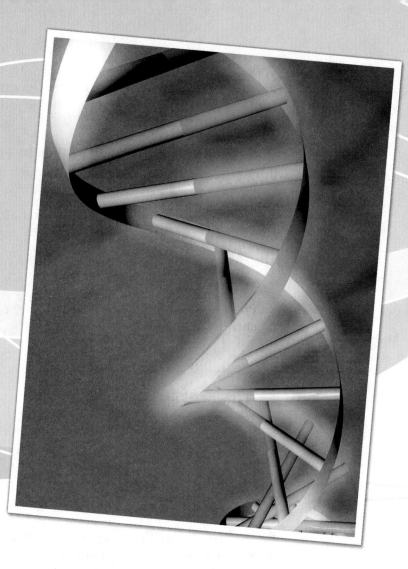

Did You Know?

promote encourage

Eugenics (from the Greek meaning "good birth") is a social philosophy that **promotes** the use of negative and/or positive interventions to perfect the human species.

compulsory mandatory

Negative eugenic interventions include **compulsory** sterilization, birth control, marriage restrictions, genetic segregation, genetic screening, abortion and infanticide.

pregnancy gestation period

Positive eugenic interventions include forced **pregnancies**, modern reproductive technologies (in vitro fertilization, egg transplants, cloning, etc.) and genetic modification.

There are three types of eugenics implementation:
1. mandatory
2. promotional
3. private

With mandatory implementation, the government mandates a eugenics program. Nazi Germany mandated a **heinous** eugenics program which included forced pregnancies, genetic "experimentation" on living human beings, mass sterilization and mass extermination.

heinous monstrous

With promotional implementation, eugenic interventions are encouraged but not mandated. In North America, women expecting children with genetic abnormalities are often subtly encouraged to abort.

With private implementation, individuals or groups voluntarily implement eugenic interventions. In some cultures, male children are preferred to female children; in such cultures, female feticide and female infanticide are practised.

At the centre of the controversy surrounding eugenic interventions is a lack of consensus as to what constitutes a genetic defect that needs to be eliminated from the human **gene pool**. Is Down syndrome a genetic defect? Cystic fibrosis? Colour blindness? Shortness? Baldness? Gender? Sexual orientation? Where exactly does society *draw the line*?

gene pool all genes of a population

Without a doubt, eugenic interventions raise serious ethical concerns for both supporters and detractors alike. In this unit, you will be asked to consider these concerns carefully and decide where you stand on the issue of eugenic interventions.

Eugenic interventions are right because they:	Eugenic interventions are wrong because they:
1. eliminate sickness and suffering.	1. devalue life.
2. reduce health-care costs.	2. decrease biodiversity.

What's the Buzz?

The social philosophy of eugenics is based on a belief in the perfectibility of the human species. By definition, a "perfectionist" is a demanding person—one who is satisfied with nothing less than perfection. Are you a perfectionist? Find out by completing the quiz below.

rough draft first version of a document

1. You write a 200-word composition for your English teacher. Satisfied with your **rough draft**, you rewrite the final version in pen. While rewriting the very last sentence, you make a spelling mistake. You:
   a) put a line through the misspelled word and correctly rewrite the word above the misspelled word.
   b) put some correction fluid over the word and, once the fluid is dry, correctly rewrite the word.
   c) rewrite the entire composition, this time ensuring that no mistakes are made.

tiny very small
stain mark, imperfection

2. As you leave your house for an important job interview, you take one last look at yourself in the mirror. You notice a **tiny**—almost imperceptible—**stain** on your shirt. You:
   a) walk out the door and go to your interview, without a second thought.
   b) put on a jacket to hide the stain and leave the house.
   c) change your shirt before leaving for the interview.

filthy very dirty

3. Friends call and ask if they can come over for a barbecue. You tell them you'd love to see them. After you hang up, you notice that your house is **filthy**! You:
   a) ignore the dirt. (After all, they invited themselves over!)
   b) clean only those areas your friends are likely to see—and will try to keep your friends in the backyard for most of the evening.

scrub clean by rubbing

   c) start **scrubbing** everything in sight!

4. You drop your new iPod on the ground. The iPod still works but is scratched. You are:
   a) unconcerned about the scratch.
   b) irritated about the scratch.
   c) so irritated about the scratch that you go out and buy a new one.

5. You get nine out of ten answers correct on a math test. You are:
   a) happy with your grade.
   b) satisfied with your grade—but will try to do better next time.
   c) mad at yourself for not getting ten out of ten!

Note: If most of your answers are *a*, you're definitely not a perfectionist. If most of your answers are *b*, you admire excellence—but are willing to settle for second best. If most of your answers are *c*, you are definitely a perfectionist! Your motto? "Second best is never good enough!"

Discussion

- Get into small groups.
- Consider the questions below.
- Present your findings to the rest of the class.

Note: As one group makes its presentation your teacher may intervene and ask you for *your* opinion. Be prepared.

1. In general, who is more of a perfectionist? A man or a woman? Explain your point of view.

2. Describe the perfect man. List a minimum of five physical traits and five personality traits. Does the perfect man exist?

3. Describe the perfect woman. List a minimum of five physical traits and five personality traits. Does the perfect woman exist?

Have You Read?

Helen Henderson is a columnist whose article, "'Culture of Perfection' Destroying Us," appeared in *The Toronto Star* on September 8, 2007. Ms. Henderson's article is about the rights of people with handicaps.

Before Reading

■ Read the defined words and comprehension questions before reading the article— skim the text for the main ideas and scan for answers to the questions.

VOCABULARY TIP
When looking up a word in the dictionary, don't just select the first definition you see. Many words have multiple definitions; the meaning changes according to the context in which the word is used.

READING STRATEGY
When reading a challenging article, read the entire article first without looking up every term you do not know. Then highlight sections of the text you find difficult to understand. List words whose meaning you cannot guess from the context and look them up in a dictionary. Active reading requires some work on your part; however, you will understand the article better, and you will improve your vocabulary!

While Reading

Informal spoken English and formal written English do not play by the same rules.

While many native speakers say "gonna," they would write "going to."

Parts of the article you are about to read are written in very formal academic English. Ten of the terms have been defined for you; five of the more difficult terms have simply been underlined. For each underlined term, can you guess the meaning of the term from the context in which it is used? If not, look up the word in a dictionary.

"CULTURE OF PERFECTION" DESTROYING US

BY HELEN HENDERSON

abort terminate

disability handicap

pregnant expecting a baby

An Italian woman who sought[1] to **abort** one of the twins she was expecting is at the centre of an international furor over society's attitude to children with **disabilities**.

When she was eighteen weeks **pregnant**, the thirty-eight-year-old from Milan was told that one of her twin baby girls had Down syndrome, characterized by an extra chromosome and intellectual disability. She asked doctors to abort that fetus. By mistake, they aborted the other. Subsequently, the second fetus was also aborted.

No surprise that the pro-Vatican *L'Osservatore Romano* censured the abortions, which were performed in June but made public only last month. But the newspaper also encapsulated the crux of the debate when it said the story exposes "the culture of perfection that imposes the exclusion of all that does not appear beautiful, glowing, positive, captivating."

"What remains is emptiness, the desert of a life without content, though perfectly planned," the newspaper continued.

And there you have it.

strive try very hard

In a world where biotechnology and genetic engineering **strive** for the smartest, the strongest and the most conventionally beautiful, there is less and less room for diversity.

peace serenity

Yet until society embraces diversity, we will never achieve **peace**.

And without peace, we will simply self-destruct—all of us, and sooner rather than later.

Twenty-two years ago, Toronto's Ruth Halperin gave birth to twins. Her daughter Daniella has Down syndrome. Daniella's twin brother, Jesse, does not.

"It is society that needs to be changed, not the child," says Halperin.

Daniella, who says she loves to dance, is helping at a daycare centre,[2] a work placement that is part of the vocational course she is taking at Seneca College. Jesse is in Holland, doing a semester overseas as part of his training to be a lawyer.

Halperin counts both her twins as blessings.

fierce intense

"Daniella has such a full life," she said in a telephone interview last week as her daughter got ready to welcome friends for a barbecue. She said she is shocked by the news out of Italy, where a **fierce** public debate is dominating news.

humankind humanity

"What happened in this hospital was not a medical abortion but an abortion done for the purposes of eugenics," one Italian senator is quoted as saying, referring to the philosophy, commonly associated with Nazi Germany, that **humankind** can be improved through selective reproduction.

wisdom intelligence
nurture take care of

40 Kids with disabilities are experts in **wisdom** and beauty and fortitude that come from deep inside. They **nurture** their nurturers against the fear, ignorance and closed minds that seek to block them from belonging.

If biotechnologists were smart, this is what they would be tapping in their race to "enhance" evolution.

45 The Italian mother-to-be is a victim of the cult of ignorance, spread in language that speaks volumes about attitudes. She is reported to have told the *Corriere della Sera* that she and her husband are "desperate over this terrible mistake" and were consulting lawyers.

sick unwell

The twin with Down syndrome is variously referred to in stories about the
50 incident as "the **sick** fetus" and "the wrong twin."

"We must create a different emotional environment, a culture of hope," says Keith Powell, executive director of Community Living Ontario, which advocates for the full inclusion of people identified as having intellectual disabilities. "We need an affirmative action campaign to advance the gifts
55 of people with disabilities."

Let's start right now as individuals to do the right thing.

552 words

---
1. Past tense of *seek*, meaning (in this context) "to consult"
2. Centre for preschool children

Reading Comprehension

- Respond to each of the questions.

1. How many fetuses was the Italian woman carrying? _____

2. List two characteristics of individuals with Down syndrome?

_____

_____

at the outset originally

3. At the outset, the Italian woman asked the doctors to abort the fetuses she was carrying.   TRUE ☐ FALSE ☐

4. Rewrite the following quotation in your own (simpler) words: "… the culture of perfection … imposes the exclusion of all that does not appear beautiful, glowing, positive, captivating."

_____

_____

5. The author believes that biotechnology and genetic engineering weaken biodiversity.   TRUE ☐ FALSE ☐

6. Circle the letter(s) of the correct answer(s). More than one response is possible.
According to the author, society:
a) should support diversity.
b) can only have peace once it supports diversity.
c) will eventually destroy itself if it cannot find peace.

7. Which word does Ruth Halperin use to describe her twins? What does this word mean?

_____

_____

8. Which word does the author define as, "… the philosophy … that humankind can be improved through selective reproduction."

_____

9. The author believes that children with disabilities have much to teach society.　　TRUE ☐　FALSE ☐

10. Which statement best summarizes the main idea of the article?
a) People with disabilities should be appreciated, not eliminated.
b) Eugenics is a philosophy most associated with Nazi Germany.
c) The Italian woman who aborted her fetuses did the wrong thing.
d) Abortion is a controversial issue.

Reading Discussion

- In small groups, discuss your answers to each of the questions below.
- Be prepared to share your group's ideas with the rest of the class.

1. Do children have the right to be born without disabilities? Explain your answer.

2. What can people with disabilities teach people without disabilities?

3. How would you *feel* if you discovered that your fetus had Down syndrome? What would you *do*?

Word Work

In the previous section, ten terms were defined for you:

Adjectives	Nouns	Verbs
1. fierce	4. disability	8. abort
2. pregnant	5. humankind	9. nurture
3. sick	6. ~~peace~~	10. strive
	7. wisdom	

- Reread the definitions provided for these words. Then reread the sentences in which the words are used to ensure that you understand how each word is used in context.

- Fill in the blanks using the listed words. The first one has been done for you as an example.

1. Can you imagine a world where there is no war—only ____peace____?

2. Catherine is in a wheelchair; however, she doesn't let her _____ stop her from participating in sports.

3. I am feeling _____: My head hurts, I have a temperature and I can't stop shaking.

4. If you fail, _____ to succeed.

5. Is your wife _____? Yes, we are expecting twins.

6. Most scientists agree that _____ is largely responsible for global warming.

7. Parents must _____ a child: They must feed, clothe, house and—most importantly—love a child.

8. Theologian Reinhold Niebuhr is credited with writing the "Serenity Prayer," the first line of which is, "God grant me the serenity to accept the things I cannot change, courage to change the things I can, and the _____ to know the difference."

9. There was a _____ storm last night; several trees were uprooted and the roof blew off my neighbour's house.

10. Women who _____ a pregnancy do so for a variety of reasons.

Have You Heard?

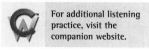

For additional listening practice, visit the companion website.

In 2006, CBC-TV's program *Our World* aired reporter Adrienne Arsenault's segment about the abortion of female fetuses in India. Guests include Ena Singh and Dr. Sabu George.

Pre-watching Vocabulary

■ Match each term with its definition. The first one has been done for you as an example.

Terms		Definitions
1. bribe (v.)	_f_	a) wedding gift from the bride and her family to the husband and his family
2. burden (n.)	___	
3. dowry (n.)	___	b) intense
4. grasp (v.)	___	c) home for children with no parents
5. helpless (adj.)	___	d) way of thinking
6. keen (adj.)	___	e) objective
7. mindset (n.)	___	f) monetary incentive to persuade someone to do something
8. orphanage (n.)	___	
9. target (n.)	___	g) understand
10. trafficking (n.)	___	h) powerless and vulnerable
		i) illegal buying and selling
		j) big, unwanted responsibility

VOCABULARY TIP
Words that sound alike but are different in spelling and in meaning are called "homophones": *aloud* means "audibly" while *allowed* means "permitted."

While Watching

You will watch the report twice.

- ▬ **The first time, listen for the general idea.**
- ▬ **The second time, listen for the details, taking point-form notes to help you remember the information.**

Watching Comprehension

▬ **Referring to your notes, respond to each of the questions below.**

1. Fill in the blanks. "_____ from Delhi and seemingly _____ back in time, Singpura is a tiny feudal village with ancient unchanging values."

2. Circle the letter(s) of the correct answer(s). More than one response is possible.
   In Singpura, India,
   a) men are in charge.
   b) women are fighting for equal rights.
   c) boys are considered a gift.
   d) girls are considered a burden.

3. Why is the woman with the hidden face considered a criminal?

   _____

   _____

   _____

4. Fill in the blanks. "Still many defend the decision to avoid having girls. 'What can we do? We're helpless. Will the government give us money for the _____?' he asks."

5. What two factors are making female feticide "easy"?
   a) _____
   b) _____

6. Female feticide is mainly a problem with the poor and uneducated of India.   TRUE ☐ FALSE ☐

7. Of the twenty new arrivals at the Delhi orphanage, how many are girls?

   _____

8. Why did the police temporarily shut down the Kohli Imaging and Diagnostic Centre?

   _____

   _____

→

9. Circle the letter(s) of the correct answer(s). More than one response is possible. According to Dr. Sabu George, what are the possible consequences of female feticide and the resulting shortage of Indian women?
   a) increased violence
   b) increased trafficking
   c) kidnapping
   d) social collapse

10. Which statement best summarizes the main idea of the report?
    a) Female feticide is illegal in India.
    b) Education is the best way to stop female feticide in India.
    c) Doctors who reveal the sex of a fetus should face harsher penalties.
    d) Ultrasound testing has increased the incidence of female feticide in India.

Would You Write That Down?

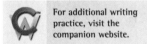
For additional writing practice, visit the companion website.

Your teacher may ask you to complete one or both of the writing activities below. If asked to write an essay, be sure to structure your writing clearly.

Free-form Writing

■ Write a 50- to 65-word paragraph in response to one of the following questions:

1. Aristotle claimed that, "Pleasure in the job puts perfection in the work." What did he mean by this? Do you agree or disagree? Justify your response.

2. Describe one "perfect moment" in your life. Be sure to use the past tense in your description.

3. Describe a person you know who has a disability. What is the disability? Was the person born with the disability? If not, how did the person become disabled? What effect does the disability have on his (or her) life? How do others react to the disability?

WRITING SUGGESTION
Writer's block occurs when you sit down to write—and your mind goes blank! One way to overcome writer's block is to brainstorm ideas (alone or with a couple of friends). Brainstorming involves writing down all your ideas—even the "bad ones," then taking a break. When you're refreshed, review your ideas and eliminate the ones you don't want to include in your writing.

Essay Writing

■ Write a 200- to 250-word essay on one of the following thesis statements. Your teacher may assign a thesis statement (and position) or allow you to select your own.

■ Do some research on the Internet to find evidence that supports your thesis statement. (See Appendix A on pages 178–187 to review the structure of a persuasive essay.)

1. Parents should (or should not) be allowed to select the gender of their children.

2. Aborting a disabled fetus is (or is not) wrong.

3. Eugenics will (or will not) lead to social inequalities.

4. Parents should (or should not) be allowed to select the sexual orientation of their offspring.

5. Society's notion of perfection is (or is not) culturally determined.

Would You Speak Up?

For additional speaking practice, visit the companion website.

Your teacher may ask you to participate in one or more of the following speaking activities.

Discussion

- In small groups, consider one (or more) of the following questions.
- Be prepared to share your thoughts with other groups in the class.

1. The following is a Chinese proverb: "The gem cannot be polished without friction, nor man perfected without trials." What does this proverb mean? Do you agree or disagree? Explain.

pros and cons advantages and disadvantages

2. What are the **pros and cons** of being a perfectionist? List at least five points.

3. In your opinion, can North Americans do anything to stop female feticide in other countries? If so, what can they do? If not, why not?

4. Would you rather have an extremely intelligent child or a child of average intelligence? Explain your choice.

looks appearance

5. Would you rather have an extraordinarily attractive child or a child of average **looks**? Explain your choice.

Discourse

- Prepare a structured, three-minute speech on one of the following thesis statements. (See Appendix B on pages 188–190 for a suggested speech structure.)
- Do some research to find evidence that supports your chosen thesis statement.
- Make sure your speech has an introduction, a development and a conclusion.

1. Parents should (or should not) be allowed to enhance their children's appearance through genetic engineering.

2. North Americans should (or should not) boycott countries where female feticide is practised.

SPEAKING SUGGESTION
Are you nervous about speaking in public because you don't want to make a mistake? Relax! Nobody's perfect. (Not even you!) Making a mistake is great when seen as an opportunity to learn something new.

3. North American society is (or is not) prejudiced against people with disabilities.

4. Prenatal testing should (or should not) be banned.

5. The eugenics movement is (or is not) a racist movement.

Debate

▬ Debate the following proposal: Eugenic interventions are wrong. (See Appendix B on pages 190–193 for the rules of debate.)

What's That Word Mean Again?

In the reading and listening sections, we focused on twenty terms—ten from each section. The activity below is designed to help you review some of this vocabulary.

Vocabulary Activity: Flash Cards

tried-and-true proved to be good

Flash cards are a **tried-and-true** method of vocabulary review.

Required
- Pen or pencil
- Twenty index cards
- A bit of time!

Instructions
1. Starting with the reading in Section B of this unit (pp. 130–131), write each of the ten terms in **bold** print on one side of an index card and the term's corresponding definition on the other side of the card.

2. Turning to the listening activity in Section B of this unit (p. 134), write each of the ten vocabulary terms on one side of an index card and the term's corresponding definition on the other side of the card.

3. Shuffle the cards and hold the pile of index cards "definition side up."

4. Read each definition and try to guess the defined word.

5. Give yourself a score out of twenty.

6. Repeat the activity until you have a perfect score!

Suggestion: Instead of reading the definitions yourself, have a partner read the definitions to you. This is a good way to practise your listening comprehension while reviewing and improving your vocabulary.

In this section, you are asked to work with another student on a project.

Project Overview

An "editorial" is an article in a publication that expresses the opinion of the editor. An "op-ed" is a signed article in a publication that expresses the opinion of a reader. (As the term implies, an op-ed is normally published on the page opposite the editorial page.) For this project, you will each write an op-ed piece on the subject of human cloning. Once each op-ed piece has been written, you will edit each other's work. Finally, you will submit your op-ed pieces to your teacher for evaluation.

Note: Use a word processor to write your op-ed pieces—and don't forget to use a spellchecker!

Writing an Op-Ed Piece

A good op-ed piece is informative, entertaining and succinct. Here are some suggestions:

1. Tell some kind of story related to the subject matter: a personal story or current event.

2. Provide general information about the subject: arguments in favour of human cloning and arguments opposed to.

3. Give your point of view on the subject: use examples to support your point of view.

4. Make a specific recommendation.

5. Include a byline, a one-sentence description of who you are: "Jane Doe is a science student at a Montreal-area college."

6. Title your work.

7. Whenever possible, use humour!

Pretend you are writing to a good friend whose opinion about the subject is the opposite of yours: try to convince your friend that your opinion is the right one!

Peer Editing

Peer editing is a three-step process that involves complimenting, suggesting and correcting:

4. Make compliments: story or current event, word choice, organization, use of humour, etc.

5. Make suggestions: more evocative vocabulary, shorter (or longer) sentences, improved focus, etc.

6. Make corrections: spelling, punctuation and grammar.

Submission

Retype your edited op-ed pieces, making sure to double-space and leave a 2.5 cm margin. Submit your project to your teacher.

Are We Too Protected?

Are you concerned about your safety? Are you afraid of falling victim to a terrorist attack or of contracting some contagious disease? Many North Americans are.

Since September 11, 2001, governments in North America and around the world have increased security measures to protect their populations and since the early 1800s, governments have passed laws requiring vaccination.

Both public security and mandatory vaccination are important issues— issues which will be explored in this unit.

It's for your own protection, sir.

SECTION A

Public Security

Examines increased security measures since 9/11.

SECTION B

Vaccination

Examines mandatory vaccination.

Public Security

Did You Know?

Terrorism is the use of violence to advance political, religious, ideological and/or territorial agendas.

On December 18, 2001, the Canadian parliament passed the *Anti-terrorism Act*.

According to a *CBC News* report, the act:
- allows for preventative arrests;
- allows for the designation of certain groups as terrorist groups;
- allows judges to force witnesses to **testify** in an investigation;
- allows suspects to be detained without charge for up to three days;
- facilitates the use of electronic equipment by police authorities;
- increases police powers.

testify give evidence

On its website, the Canadian Department of Justice lists several recent terrorist acts:
- the bombing of the World Trade Towers in 2001;
- the Bali discotheque bombing in 2002;
- the Madrid train station bombing in 2004;
- the Russian school tragedy in 2004;
- the London **transit** bombing in 2005.

transit public transportation

The department points to these acts as justification for Canada's anti-terrorism legislation, stating that "no country, including Canada, is immune."

Regardless of these terrorist acts and the possibility of one taking place in Canada, many Canadians are concerned about increased security measures, believing that these measures violate **civil rights**. In response to the installation of closed circuit television (CCTV) security cameras in Canada, Alan Borovoy of the Canadian Civil Liberties Association stated that "citizens in a free country should have a presumptive right to get lost ... to **wander around** without government **keeping tabs on us**."

civil rights basic human rights

wander around move around with no particular destination

keep tabs on somebody watch somebody closely

So what do you think? Are current public security measures appropriate or inappropriate? Once again, it's up to you to decide.

Current public security measures are right because they:	Current public security measures are wrong because they:
1. reassure the public.	1. encourage paranoia.
2. counteract terrorism.	2. are intrusive.

Turn to page 155 for a cooperative project based on this introductory reading.

What's the Buzz?

The following are five hypothetical situations, each of which raises an important question.

- In pairs or small groups, respond to all five questions.
- Be prepared to share your answers with the class.

put up with tolerate

1. For years, downtown residents have **put up with** drug selling and prostitution in their neighbourhood. A small group has organized a petition calling for the installation of CCTV security cameras. There are more than 5,000 names on the petition. You are the mayor. Do you comply with the petition? Why or why not?

_____

_____

comings and goings activities

2. You live in a downtown neighbourhood that has recently installed CCTV security cameras. Are you concerned that all your **comings and goings** are being filmed? Why or why not?

_____

_____

3. The government is proposing the implementation of a microchip identification program: Every Canadian would have a microchip with his or her personal identification number implanted under the skin. The government will hold a referendum on the question. You are a Canadian voter. Would you support the proposal? Why or why not?

_____

_____

overhear accidentally hear
hijack forcibly take control of a vehicle

4. While waiting for a flight, you **overhear** the couple behind you joking about **hijacking** the plane. Do you inform officials? Why or why not?

_____

_____

takeoff airplane departure

5. Minutes before **takeoff**, you get a "funny feeling" that something is wrong: the two men beside you are talking in hushed voices and one of them seems very nervous. Would you get off the plane? Why or why not?

_____

_____

Have You Read?

For additional reading practice, visit the companion website.

In the article you're about to read, columnist Les MacPherson takes a humorous look at present anti-terrorist security measures. Mr. MacPherson's article appeared in Saskatoon's _The Star Phoenix_ on August 22, 2006.

Before Reading

VOCABULARY TIP
The adjectives _naked_ and _nude_ are synonyms meaning "wearing no clothes." However, _nude_ is typically used in an artistic context: The artist's model was nude.

■ Read the defined words and comprehension questions before reading the article—skim the text for the main ideas and scan for answers to the questions.

While Reading

■ Refer to the pictures on page 145 as you read the article; the graphic support will help your understanding.

READING STRATEGY
Have you ever had a difficult time understanding a text? Sometimes, viewing information graphically can help. For example, organizing information in a chart—or even drawing a picture—can help you understand better.

EXPLODING PANTS MIGHT GIVE TERRORISTS IDEAS

BY LES MACPHERSON

When it comes to television, I have only one rule: If a show about exploding pants comes on, I'm watching it.

delight joy

Imagine my **delight**, then, when just such a show came on the other evening. This was an episode of *Mythbusters*,[1] a series I like to watch even when it
5 doesn't feature exploding pants.

blend combine
blow up explode

Broadcast on the Discovery Channel, *Mythbusters* **blends** science and entertainment in a way that often involves **blowing** things **up**. The series features a team of Hollywood special-effects experts who test the veracity of various urban myths. Their experiments are typically preceded by

shout yell
ignite set on fire

10 someone **shouting**, "Fire in the hole!" To test an oft-told popular myth about a tragic bathroom explosion, for example, the *Mythbusters* **ignited** a toilet filled with gasoline under a crash-test dummy. Their conclusion: Do not try this at home.

Featured on the show the other evening was a myth about exploding
15 pants. This one originates in New Zealand, way back in the 1930s.

According to news accounts of the day, a number of farmers were injured when, without warning, their pants exploded. One was actually killed and several others injured. The prevailing theory was that their pants were impregnated with farm chemicals that detonated when exposed to an
20 ignition source.

The *Mythbusters* confirmed that this was indeed possible. Jeans impregnated with a herbicide widely used in New Zealand at the time did indeed go up in a fireball when ignited. The dummy wearing the pants was badly singed.

25 As usual, the *Mythbusters* continued the experiment beyond the point of science and into the realm of good, old, blowing-things-up fun. This time they had their dummy, Buster, dressed in pants smeared with some kind of high-explosive gel. Detonated by remote control from a distant block-house, these pants exploded with a *BANG* violent enough to shake the

blast explosion

30 cameras. The unfortunate Buster was disintegrated in the **blast**.

This was television at its finest. Critics are saying the episode has a lock on this year's Emmy award[2] for best exploding pants.

evil bad

What has me worried is the possibility that exploding pants might be used for **evil** instead of entertainment. It occurs to me that, if the *Mythbusters* can
35 make exploding pants, so can terrorists. This might be the ruse they're looking for to sneak explosives onto a jet airliner.

They already tried with explosives concealed in a would-be suicide bomber's shoes. That's why air travellers must now remove their shoes for pre-flight inspection. More recently, authorities foiled a terrorist plot to bring down
40 multiple jet airliners using explosive liquids disguised as toiletries. As a result, legitimate passengers can no longer take liquids onto the plane.

threat menace

trousers pants

worldwide global

We don't need to guess what new security measures will be imposed in the event of a terrorist **threat** involving explosive pants.

45 Before we get on the plane, we'll have to surrender our **trousers** along with our nail files and our bottled water.

One more reason to wear clean underwear when you travel.

Of course, it won't stop there. If pants can be made to explode, so can any other garment, even skivvies.[3] To ensure that such things are not brought onto a plane, we'll all have to fly naked. This could have a profound, 50 **worldwide** effect on commercial aviation. A lot of people would rather travel by bus than fly starkers.[4] Others, however, might want to fly more often. Maybe they'd balance out.

Either way, at least passengers would be safe from pants bombers.

Naked, shivering and safe.

578 words

1. Popular TV show
2. American TV award
3. Informal term for underwear
4. Informal term for naked

Reading Comprehension

▬ Respond to each of the questions below.

1. What is the main objective of the TV show *Mythbusters*?

_____

2. How long has the exploding-pants myth been around?

_____

3. In your own words, what theoretical explanation was given for the New Zealand farmers' exploding pants?

_____

_____

_____

4. The *Mythbusters* team exploded a dummy's pants twice. How and why did they do it the first time? The second time?

_____

_____

_____

_____

_____

5. Why is the author worried about the exploding pants?

_____

_____

_____

6. In the past, where have terrorists tried to conceal explosives when boarding a plane? List two places.

a) _____

b) _____

7. What impact did the discovery of these concealed explosives (see previous question) have on airline passengers?

a) _____

b) _____

8. According to the author, what will happen to airline passengers if terrorists are caught with exploding pants?

_____

_____

9. The author humourously concludes that if pants can be made to explode, so too can underwear. What impact would exploding underwear have on passengers?

_____

10. Which statement best summarizes the main idea of the article?
a) Exploding pants are a serious threat to airline passenger safety.
b) Anti-terrorist security measures need to be increased.
c) The TV show *Mythbusters* is extremely violent.
d) There are limits to what can and should be done to ensure airline passenger safety.

Discussion

▬ In pairs or small groups, discuss your answers to each of the questions below.

▬ Be prepared to share your thoughts with the class.

1. Are you concerned about your safety when travelling by plane? If so, what are your concerns? If not, why not?

2. Why do many TV viewers enjoy watching things blow up?

3. In your opinion, is the government doing enough to protect citizens from terrorism?

Word Work

In the previous section, ten terms were defined for you:

Adjective	Nouns	Verbs
1. worldwide	2. blast 3. delight 4. evil 5. threat 6. trousers	7. blend 8. blow up 9. ~~ignite~~ 10. shout

■ Each of the sentences below contains a term in italics. Choose a term from the list above that could replace the italicized term and not change the meaning of the sentence.

■ Conjugate all verbs correctly.

■ Try doing the exercise *without looking back* at the definitions provided in the reading section. The first one has been done for you as an example.

Answer

1. An arsonist *sets* things *on fire*.   *ignites*

2. Do you take the terrorist *menace* seriously?   _____

3. Due to a gas leak, the house *exploded*.   _____

4. Her tastes are eclectic; she *combines* the modern with the antique.   _____

5. His little girl is a *joy*! She is always laughing.   _____

6. I can't find *pants* to match my shirt.   _____

7. Stop *yelling*! I am not deaf.   _____

8. The British royal family are *global* travellers.   _____

9. There is both good and *bad* in this world.   _____

10. There was a huge *explosion* at the gas station.   _____

Have You **H**eard?

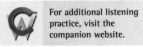

For additional listening practice, visit the companion website.

commuter person who travels from home to work

On July 7, 2005, four suicide bombers attacked the London underground system, killing 52 **commuters** and injuring 700. Later that day, CBC aired correspondent Susan Ormiston's report entitled "The List," a reference to Al-Qaeda leader Osama bin Laden's 2002 list of six targeted countries: Great Britain, France, Italy, Germany, Australia and Canada. Ms. Ormiston's guests include Colin Kenny, chair of the Senate Committee on National Security; Eric Margolis, Foreign Affairs Analyst; Michel Juneau-Katsuya, former CSIS Agent; Anne McLellan, the Minister of Public Safety in 2005; Derek Humble, a security consultant with Total Security Management; and Toronto commuters. CBC anchor Peter Mansbridge introduces the report. .

Pre-watching Vocabulary

Below you will find ten idiomatic expressions, phrasal verbs and collocations.

- Match each expression with the correct explanation. The first one has been done for you as an example.
- You may wish to use a dictionary to complete this exercise.

Expressions		Explanations
1. be spared (from) something	_i_	a) brutal method
2. contingency plan	_____	b) not differentiate
3. draw no distinction	_____	c) insult
4. issue a warning	_____	d) not get involved in something
5. ruthless tactic	_____	e) emergency plan
6. sense of security	_____	f) common frontier
7. shared border	_____	g) feeling of safety
8. slap in the face	_____	h) actions which are suspect
9. stay out of something	_____	i) not have to endure something
10. suspicious activities	_____	j) make a public, cautionary statement

While Watching

You will watch segment twice.

- The first time you watch, try to understand the speakers' positions on Canadian security and terrorist groups.
- The second time, listen for the details of what each speaker has to say, taking point-form notes to help you remember the information.

Watching Comprehension

While you are watching, respond to each of the questions.

1. Fill in the blanks. "All the emergency measures in the world can't prepare people. An attack like the one in London always comes as a shock. Londoners have never doubted they are a target. Security in their city has been tight for decades. They know what it's like to see armed soldiers in their airports. For the most part, Canadians _____ _____ _____ that. But Al Qaeda has identified this country as a target. So why aren't we worried?" (Peter Mansbridge)

2. Colin Kenny suggests that Canadians have a false sense of security. TRUE ☐ FALSE ☐

3. When was Spain added to Al-Qaeda's list of six targeted countries? What terrorist attack occurred in Spain?

   _____

   _____

4. Circle the letter(s) of the correct answer(s). More than one response is possible.
   According to Eric Margolis, Canada is:
   a) at risk.
   b) next on the list.
   c) a pretty soft target (because it is not that difficult to get into and has got a mixed ethnic population).
   d) a nice, decent, country.

5. Fill in the blanks. "Canada _____ _____ _____ the Iraqi war, which may have insulated us. But we are fighting together with the United States in Afghanistan, and that exposes us." (Susan Ormiston)

6. Michel Juneau-Katsuya theorizes that a terrorist attack in Canada would result in a shutdown of the Canadian-U.S. border, making it more difficult for terrorists to launch another attack on the U.S. TRUE ☐ FALSE ☐

7. After the terrorist attack in Spain, Anne McLellan tried to reassure Canadian commuters by announcing that new (security) systems had been put into place. List the two systems mentioned.

   a) _____

   b) _____

8. Fill in the blanks. "I know there's departments like emergency procedures, like _____ _____ in place, but as average Canadians, we don't know what they are. Like ... do we know if it's enough?" (unidentified Toronto commuter)

---

9. According to Derek Humble, what is the only thing protecting Canada from a terrorist attack right now?

_____

_____

10. Which statement best summarizes the main idea of the report?
   a) A terrorist attack on Canada is imminent.
   b) There are more than fifty terror groups in Canada.
   c) Canadians should not be complacent about terrorism in Canada.
   d) Current Canadian security measures are insufficient in the fight against terrorism.

Would You Write That Down?

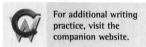

Your teacher may ask you to complete one or more of the following writing activities.

Free-form Writing

▬ Write a 50- to 65-word paragraph in response to one of the following questions:

1. A school bully is a child who terrorizes his or her classmates. In your opinion, what's the best way to deal with a school bully?

2. Do you enjoy watching movies in which things are blown up? Why or why not?

3. Are you willing to sacrifice personal freedom for security? Explain.

Essay Writing

▬ Write a 200- to 250-word essay on one of the following thesis statements. Your teacher may assign a thesis statement (and position) or allow you to select your own.

▬ Do some research on the Internet to find evidence that supports your thesis statement. (See Appendix A on pages 178–187 to review the structure of a persuasive essay.)

1. Cyber-terrorism is (or is not) a serious threat to national security.

2. Closed circuit television (CCTV) security cameras should (or should not) be banned from public streets.

3. Eco-sabotage[5] is (or is not) justifiable.

---

5. Violence against property carried out by environmental activists (sometimes referred to as eco-terrorism).

4. Individuals convicted of terrorist acts should (or should not) receive the death penalty.

5. Security measures in Canadian airports are (or are not) sufficient.

Would You Speak Up?

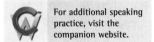
For additional speaking practice, visit the companion website.

Your teacher may ask you to participate in one or more of the following speaking activities.

Discussion

▬ In small groups, consider one (or more) of the following questions.
▬ Be prepared to share your thoughts with other groups in the class.

1. Are you concerned about being the victim of a terrorist act when you use mass transit? Why or why not?

2. Most public places such as schools and shopping centres have CCTV security cameras. When you are in public places, are you aware of these cameras? If so, how do they make you feel?

3. A smart card is a plastic card with an embedded microchip that stores personal information. In your opinion, should citizens be forced to carry "smart" identification cards at all times? Why or why not?

4. Are you prepared for a national emergency? Explain.

5. American President Franklin D. Roosevelt said that "... the only thing we have to fear is fear itself ...." Explain this statement in your own words. Illustrate your explanation with an example.

Discourse

▬ Prepare a structured, three-minute speech on one of the thesis statements below. (See Appendix B on pages 188–190 for a suggested speech structure.)
▬ Do some research to find evidence that supports your chosen thesis statement.
▬ Make sure your speech has an introduction, a development and a conclusion.

1. The *Anti-terrorism Act* violates (or does not violate) civil rights.

2. Using microchip identification on humans is (or is not) desirable.

3. The installation of CCTV security cameras reduces (or does not reduce) crime.

4. Airline passengers should (or should not) be allowed to have carry-on luggage.

5. Canada is (or is not) immune to terrorism.

Debate

▬ Debate the following proposal: Current public security measures are wrong. (See Appendix B on pages 190–193 for the rules of debate.)

What's That Word Mean Again?

In the reading and listening sections, we focused on twenty terms—ten from each section. The activity below is designed to help you review some of this vocabulary.

Vocabulary Activity: Word Bingo!

Bingo is a fun way to win prizes and revise vocabulary. If you've got some spare time, why not play a game?

Required
• Pens or pencils
• Blank sheets of paper
• Twenty small slips of paper (or index cards)
• A hat
• Bingo tokens (or pennies)
• A minimum of five players
• A "caller" (your teacher?)
• Some prizes

Instructions
1. On a blank sheet of paper, each player creates a four-by-four grid. (See illustration on page 155.)

2. In each of the sixteen squares, players write down a vocabulary term from this section of the unit. Players select eight terms from the reading section (p. 149) and eight terms from the watching section (p. 150).

3. On each of the twenty slips of paper, the caller writes down a vocabulary term from this section of the unit (see pages 149 and 150.)

4. The caller places the twenty slips of paper in a hat.

5. The caller randomly selects a slip of paper from the hat and reads the vocabulary term aloud.

6. Players place a token on the corresponding vocabulary term in their grids.

7. Steps 5 and 6 are repeated until one of the players has placed four tokens in a row (horizontally, vertically or diagonally).

8. The first player to get four in a row says "Bingo" and wins the prize.

Suggestion: Repeat the activity; this time, the winning player has to explain the meaning of the four terms that gave him or her a "bingo" in order to collect the prize. If he or she can't correctly explain the terms, no prize is given and the game continues.

draw no distinction	slap in the face	ignite	ruthless tactic
blast	suspicious activities	evil	threat
stay out of something	delight	issue a warning	shared border
blend	sense of security	blow up	shout

Would You Like to Work Together?

In this section, you are asked to work with another student on a speaking project.

Project Overview

In the "Did You Know?" section of this part of the unit, you read an **overview** article about terrorism and public security measures in Canada (pp. 142–143). One way to summarize an article and assimilate information is to write questions, the answers to which are found in the article you are reading. Take for example the first sentence of the "Did You Know?" article, "Terrorism is the use of violence to advance political, religious, ideological and/or territorial agendas."

A question you could write based on the information contained in this sentence would be, "What is terrorism?" Working with a partner, you will create ten questions based on the "Did You Know?" article; then you will ask these questions to another team of two in the class.

Procedure
This activity is carried out in two parts.

Part A
1. Working with your chosen (or assigned) partner, create ten questions based on the "Did You Know?" article. Note: Use a combination of "yes/no" and "information questions." Use at least two different tenses when writing your questions. (To review question formation, see *Parallels: Exploring the Issues English Grammar*.) After each question, name the tense used (simple present, present continuous, simple past, past continuous, etc.)

double-check verify by checking a second time

2. **Double-check** your question formation and submit your list of questions to your teacher for verification.

Part B
3. With your partner, challenge another team of two to correctly respond to your teacher-verified list of questions. Note: You must read (not show) your questions to the opposing team and neither team may look back at the original article.

4. Give one point for each correct answer and zero points for each incorrect answer. If you're unsure about the answer, ask your teacher to act as "referee."

5. Alternate asking and answering questions with the other team.

6. The team with the highest score wins!

Variation: Your teacher may increase the difficulty of this project by selecting two new articles on terrorism and public security and giving copies of the articles to all teams of two. All teams read both articles. Half of the teams write questions based on Article A and half of the teams write questions based on Article B. The "challenge" is then carried out as described in Part B above, pairing Article A teams with Article B teams.

Vaccination

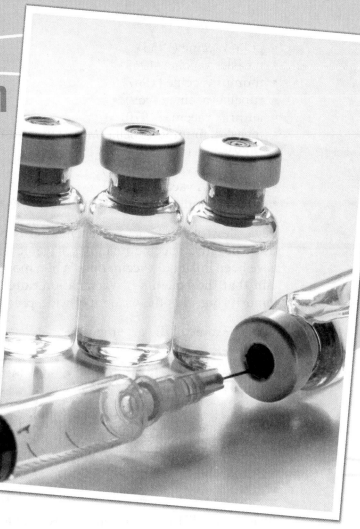

 Did You Know?

strain form
antibody protein that fights infection

A vaccine is a preparation containing weakened or dead **strains** of a microbe that causes disease. An individual is injected with this preparation, stimulating the immune system to produce **antibodies**.

smallpox variola, a highly contagious viral disease

British physician Edward Jenner is credited with the development of the first vaccine in the late 1700s when in 1796 he inoculated an eight-year-old boy with the **smallpox** virus. Thanks to Jenner's discovery and subsequent vaccination programs in the nineteenth and twentieth centuries, humankind succeeded in eliminating smallpox from nature by 1977; to this day, smallpox remains the only disease to have been eliminated in this way.

timeline chronology

Vaccines exist for a myriad of diseases. The website keepkidshealthy.com provides an exhaustive list presented on an immunization **timeline**. Here are some of the more recent highlights:

- polio vaccine (1955)
- measles vaccine (1963)
- mumps vaccine (1967)
- rubella vaccine (1969)
- anthrax vaccine (1970)
- measles, mumps, rubella (MMR) vaccine (1971)
- **flu** vaccine (1978)
- hepatitis B vaccine (1982)
- hepatitis A vaccine (1995)
- human papilloma virus (HPV) vaccine (2006)

flu widespread viral disease

Regardless of the benefits, vaccination is not without short- and long-term risks: negative vaccine reactions have occurred, and some chronic diseases have been linked to vaccination. While most in the medical community maintain that the benefits of vaccination outweigh the risks, a small but vocal minority question the wisdom of widespread mandatory vaccination.

Here are some of the arguments:

Mandatory vaccination is right because it:	Mandatory vaccination is wrong because it:
1. is economical.	1. violates freedom of choice.
2. saves lives.	2. is potentially unsafe.

Turn to page 171 for a cooperative project based on this introductory reading.

What's the Buzz?

The following are five hypothetical situations, each of which raises an important question.

- In pairs or small groups, respond to all five questions.
- Be prepared to share your answers with the class.

advocate recommend

1. You are a doctor who belongs to a religious group that **advocates** abstinence from sex before marriage. Your patient, a twelve-year-old girl, asks you for the HPV vaccine. HPV is a disease that can only be contracted sexually. Do you vaccinate her, or do you refer her to a colleague? Explain your decision.

_____

_____

measles disease characterized by small red spots all over the body

2. A young child dies because his parents refused to have him vaccinated against **measles**. The parents' religion prohibits vaccination. Are the parents guilty of physical neglect? Why or why not?

_____

_____

liver organ that cleans the blood

needle syringe

3. Hepatitis B is a serious disease in which a virus attacks the **liver**; potential consequences of hepatitis B include infection, cirrhosis of the liver, liver cancer, liver failure and death. Hepatitis B is spread through the blood (sexual contact, **needle** sharing and childbirth). Multiple sclerosis has been linked to the hepatitis B vaccine. If you were in danger of getting hepatitis B, would you be vaccinated? Why or why not?

_____

_____

chicken pox viral disease, varicella

4. Your six-year-old child is terrified of needles: she throws a tantrum every time she is vaccinated. A **chicken pox** vaccine exists. Do you have her vaccinated, or do you simply let her contract the disease? Explain your decision.

_____

_____

5. The influenza vaccine is recommended for people with certain chronic diseases as well as babies, the elderly and those working with these populations. You are a young and healthy eighteen-year-old. Would you get the influenza vaccination? Why or why not?

_____

_____

Have You Read?

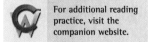

For additional reading practice, visit the companion website.

In the article you're about to read, physician Gifford Jones writes about his personal battle with polio. Dr. Jones's article appeared in *The Sault Star* on July 30, 2005.

Before Reading

■ Read the defined words and comprehension questions before reading the article—skim the text for the main ideas and scan for answers to the questions.

Refer to the pictures on page 160 as you read the article; the graphic support will help your understanding.

TWELVE HOURS LATER I COULDN'T RAISE MY LEGS— POLIO NIGHTMARE LINGERS

BY GIFFORD JONES

Why write about polio[1] when the disease is a faint echo for most people?

It's because I developed this disease years ago when a vaccine was not available. So I've never understood why some parents still question the use of vaccines and try to withhold them from their children. Yogi Berra,[2]
5 you see, was right.

I had just started my final year at Harvard Medical School.

graduate finish school

I was in good spirits. By this time I was confident I might even **graduate**!

But one morning I awakened with a thunderous headache and I couldn't blame it on partying. Later that day I was rushed to Boston's Children's
10 Hospital and twelve hours later the virus[3] had paralyzed my legs. You never forget being told by doctors that you may never walk again.

April 12, 1955 means nothing to readers, but on that day the discovery of Salk's[4] polio vaccine was announced to the world.

It ended an era of global fear and fifty years later polio has been eradicated
15 from North America.

recall remember
outbreak occurrence

I vividly **recall** as a young child the summer fear that struck when mere whispers of a polio **outbreak** froze everyday life.

Swimming pools were closed, movie theatres emptied and front doors shut.

strike attack
cripple paralyze

Unlike today's influenza that **strikes** the elderly, polio either killed or
20 **crippled** the young.

The first polio outbreaks occurred in Europe in the nineteenth century and a few years later in North America. Between 1927 and 1962 there were 50,000 cases reported in Canada.

Later, in 1972, polio struck a Connecticut school.

25 Then, in 1977, a report in the *Canadian Medical Association Journal* showed that wild strains of the virus had been isolated from sewage dumped into the Ottawa River.

In 1993 an outbreak of polio occurred in the Netherlands with sixty-eight cases among adults and children.

30 At least two persons were known to have died.

This outbreak was traced to groups that refused immunization on religious grounds.

As recently as 1988 reports from the World Health Organization showed that 350,000 children were paralyzed with polio worldwide.

35 Today this disease is still present in Africa and Asia. Moreover, in a shrinking world, polio and other infectious diseases are a mere plane ride away.

Just by the roll of the dice some victims are fortunate enough to regain most of their muscles.

40 What we didn't realize early on was that Yogi Berra, philosopher-king of the New York Yankees, was right when he remarked during a baseball game that "it ain't over until it's over."

Now we know that twenty-five percent of those who suffered paralytic polio develop the "post-polio syndrome" twenty to thirty years later.

insidious destructive

45 It's such a slow **insidious** process that muscle changes are initially imperceptible until it starts to interfere with daily activities.

breathing respiring

Former patients may get up in the morning refreshed but feel exhausted by noon and have trouble **breathing**.

Why does this happen? Most people believe the polio virus attacks and
50 destroys muscles.

It doesn't.

spine vertebral column

Muscles contract because cells in the **spine** send messages telling them to do so and it's these cells that are either totally or partially destroyed by the virus.

55 It's believed these partially destroyed cells have to work harder and they can do so for a limited period of time. But like plugging too many appliances into an electrical outlet they eventually blow a fuse and post-polio syndrome begins.

Ironically this is one situation where "use it or lose it" doesn't apply.
60 Rather, using these muscles too much accelerates their aging and the
onset of weakness.

onset start

Today there's a tendency to believe that infectious disease is past history. After all, the smallpox that once ravaged mankind has been eradicated thanks to worldwide vaccination.

65 But infection never takes a holiday and diseases can return with a vengeance.

recover get back

I was one of the lucky ones who **recovered** most of the muscle loss.

But weeks of therapy were required before I could walk up a few stairs.

Fifty years later I have not forgotten the miracle of polio vaccine.

70 Nor the more than twelve vaccines that help to prevent serious disease.

Let's never get sloppy about prevention or refuse these vaccines to children.

706 words

1. Disease affecting brain and spinal cord
2. Famous baseball player whose comically confusing expressions are legendary
3. A sub-microscopic particle that infects the cells of a host organism. A virus cannot reproduce on its own (wikipedia.org).
4. Dr. Jonas Edward Salk, inventor of the first polio vaccine

Reading Comprehension

■ Respond to each of the questions.

1. Why did the author write an article about polio at a time when few people think about the disease?

_____

2. What was the author's first symptom that something was wrong?

_____

3. From the onset, how long did it take for paralysis to set in?

_____

4. In 2005, did polio exist in North America?   YES ☐   NO ☐

5. Prior to the discovery of the polio vaccination, how did society react to reported outbreaks?

_____

_____

_____

_____

6. In what way is polio different from today's influenza?

_____

_____

_____

7. What caused the 1993 polio outbreak in the Netherlands?

_____

_____

_____

8. How is the onset of post-polio syndrome different from the onset of paralytic polio?

_____

_____

_____

9. In your own words, how does post-polio syndrome develop?

_____

_____

_____

_____

10. Which statement best summarizes the main idea of the article?
  a) Polio is a deadly disease.
  b) Polio has been eradicated from North America.
  c) Parents must immunize their children against serious diseases.
  d) Childhood vaccination is a controversial issue.

Discussion

- In pairs or small groups, discuss your answers to each of the questions below.
- Be prepared to share your thoughts with the class.

1. Would you be able to give someone an injection? Why or why not?

2. List three common childhood viral infections. (You may wish to refer back to the "Did You Know?" section on page 157.) Describe two symptoms for each infection. Which infection is most serious? Justify your response.

3. Who makes a better patient? A man or a woman? Explain.

Word Work

In the previous section, ten terms were defined for you:

Adjective	Nouns	Verbs
1. insidious	2. breathing	6. cripple
	3. onset	7. graduate
	4. outbreak	8. recall
	5. spine	9. recover
		10. strike

- Each of the sentences on the following page contains a term in italics. Choose a term from the list above that could replace the italicized term and not change the meaning of the sentence.
- Conjugate all verbs correctly.
- Try doing the exercise _without looking back_ at the definitions provided in the reading section. The first one has been done for you as an example.

1. Do you *remember* your first vaccination?   *recall*

2. Dr. Jones was *attacked* by polio when he was a young adult.   _____

3. Children are *paralyzed* by polio.   _____

4. In 1995, an *occurrence* of the Ebola virus killed 245 people in The Congo.   _____

5. Paralysis can occur if the *vertebral column* is damaged.   _____

6. People with asthma have trouble *respiring*.   _____

7. Polio patients may *get back* the use of their legs.   _____

8. She hopes to *finish school* and get a job this year.   _____

9. Smallpox is an extremely *destructive* disease.   _____

10. The *start* of post-polio syndrome occurs twenty to thirty years after the initial infection.   _____

Have You Heard?

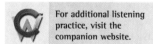

For additional listening practice, visit the companion website.

You will watch two *CTV News* segments filed by reporter Jill Macyshon.

The first segment, which aired in 2007, is about vaccinating young women against the human papilloma virus (HPV).

The second segment, which aired in 2004, is about vaccinating babies and young children against influenza.

Pre-watching Vocabulary

On the following page you will find ten idiomatic expressions, phrasal verbs and collocations.

- Match each expression with the correct explanation. The first one has been done for you as an example.
- You may wish to use a dictionary to complete this exercise.

VOCABULARY TIP

Both the common cold and the flu (influenza) are viral infections. Symptoms of a cold include sneezing, nasal congestion, coughing and headaches. Symptoms of the flu are similar to those of a cold, only more severe; the flu can sometimes be fatal. Verbs associated with viral infections include *catch* and *contract*: She caught a cold; her husband contracted the flu.

Segment 1

Expressions		Explanations
1. cover the cost	_e_	a) for reasons relating to a person's spiritual beliefs
2. It's better to be safe than sorry.	____	b) principal reason
3. leading cause	____	c) strongly encourage a person to perform an action
4. on religious grounds	____	d) It's best to be prudent.
5. urge someone to do something	____	e) pay for something

Segment 2

Expressions		Explanations
6. underway	____	f) vaccination against influenza
7. flu shot	____	h) assigned place in a schedule
8. looming pandemic	____	i) very infectious form of a virus
9. time slot	____	g) in progress
10. virulent strain	____	j) imminent infection of a large number of people

While Watching

You will watch each segment twice.

- The first time you watch, try to understand the speakers' positions on vaccination.
- The second time, listen for the details of what each speaker has to say, taking point-form notes to help you remember the information.

> **LISTENING STRATEGY**
> Before listening for information, think about what you already know about the subject. In this case, what do you know about vaccination? What words do you think will be used? Needle? Infection? Doctor? Putting yourself in the right frame of mind will help improve your understanding.

Watching Comprehension

■ **While you are watching, respond to each of the questions below:**

Segment 1

1. What percentage of the Canadian population will be infected with HPV during their lifetimes?

   _____

2. What is the possible consequence of an undetected HPV infection in women?

   _____

   _____

3. How much is an HPV vaccine?

   _____

   _____

4. Why are some parents hesitant to talk to their children about HPV vaccination?

   _____

   _____

   _____

5. Which statement best summarizes the main idea of the report?
   a) HPV can cause a deadly disease.
   b) Girls should be vaccinated against HPV.
   c) HPV vaccination should be mandatory for both males and females.
   d) The vaccination of girls for HPV is a controversial issue.

Segment 2

6. Did the doctor diagnose baby Raina with a cold or the flu?

   _____

7. Fill in the blanks. "It is better for your child to be immunized and prevent getting the disease as best you can than it is to allow your child to have the influenza, particularly if we get a very _____ _____ of influenza."

avian relating to birds

8. How many people did the **avian** flu kill the year before Jill Macyshon's report aired on *CTV News*?

   _____

9. Raina's mother does not want her child to have a flu shot.   TRUE ☐ FALSE ☐

10. Which statement best summarizes the main idea of the report?
   a) Vaccination is unnecessary.
   b) Providing at-risk Canadians with vaccinations is costly, but necessary.
   c) It is difficult to diagnose colds and flus.
   d) Canadian doctors are overworked during the flu season.

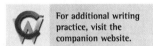

Would You Write That Down?

Your teacher may ask you to complete one or more of the following writing activities.

Free-form Writing

■ Write a 50- to 65-word paragraph in response to one of the following questions:

1. Describe the first vaccination you remember having. How old were you? Where did it take place? What were you vaccinated against? How did you feel?

get well recover

2. Describe a time when you were sick. What disease did you have? How were you treated? How did you feel? How long did it take for you to **get well**?

3. When you are getting an injection, are you able to watch? Why or why not?

WRITING SUGGESTION
Good essay writers carefully choose their main arguments. Before writing your essay, make a list of as many arguments as you can and then select the best ones.

Essay Writing

■ Write a 200- to 250-word essay on one of the following thesis statements. Your teacher may assign a thesis statement (and position) or allow you to select your own.

■ Do some research on the Internet to find evidence that supports your thesis statement. (See Appendix A on pages 178–187 to review the structure of a persuasive essay.)

1. The government should (or should not) pay for HPV vaccinations.

pet domestic animal

2. **Pets** are (or are not) over-vaccinated.

3. Drug companies charge (or do not charge) too much for vaccinations.

4. Exercise and good nutrition are (or are not) sufficient to keep people healthy.

5. Children should (or should not) get flu shots.

Would You Speak Up?

For additional speaking practice, visit the companion website.

Your teacher may ask you to participate in one or more of the following speaking activities.

Discussion

■ In small groups, consider one (or more) of the following questions.

■ Be prepared to share your thoughts with other groups in the class.

1. Is Gifford Jones's article "Twelve Hours Later I Couldn't Raise My Legs …" (pp. 161–163) objective, subjective or a mixture of both? Explain.

2. Should parents be allowed to refuse an HPV vaccination for **underage** daughters wanting to be vaccinated? Why or why not?

underage under the legal age of consent

sample specimen

3. The smallpox virus is currently stored in two laboratories: the Centers for Disease Control and Prevention (CDC) in the United States and the State Research Center of Virology and Biotechnology in Russia. Should these last remaining **samples** be destroyed? Justify your response.

overly excessively

4. Childhood vaccination has been associated with Sudden Infant Death Syndrome (SIDS). In Canada, two to three babies die from SIDS each week. If you were a parent, would you be **overly** concerned about vaccinating your baby?

spread propagation

5. We live in a global village. With modern airplanes, people can now travel great distances in short periods of time. What effects could increased travel have on the **spread** of disease? List a minimum of two effects.

Discourse

WORD CULTURE
The expression *global village* refers to the perception that the world is a smaller place due to electronic communications. Canadian educator Marshall McLuhan is credited with coining the expression.

■ Prepare a structured, three-minute speech on one of the following thesis statements. (See Appendix B on pages 188–190 for a suggested speech structure.)

■ Do some research to find evidence that supports your chosen thesis statement.

■ Make sure your speech has an introduction, a development and a conclusion.

1. Vaccination is (or is not) risky.

2. Children who are not vaccinated should (or should not) be allowed to attend public schools.

3. People with diseases for which there is no vaccination should (or should not) be quarantined.

4. Disease can (or can not) be eliminated from our world.

5. Biological warfare is (or is not) morally reprehensible.

Debate

■ Debate the following proposal: Mandatory vaccination is wrong. (See Appendix B on pages 190–193 for the rules of debate.)

What's That Word Mean Again?

In the reading and listening sections, we focused on twenty terms—ten from each section. The activity below is designed to help you review some of this vocabulary.

Vocabulary Activity: Word Bingo!

Bingo is a fun way to win prizes and revise vocabulary. If you've got some spare time, why not play a game?

Required
- Pens or pencils
- Blank sheets of paper
- Twenty small slips of paper (or index cards)
- A hat
- Bingo tokens (or pennies)
- A minimum of five players
- A "caller" (your teacher?)
- Some prizes

Instructions
1. On a blank sheet of paper, each player creates a four-by-four grid. (See illustration on page 171.)

2. In each of the sixteen squares, players write down a vocabulary term from this section of the unit. Players select eight terms from the reading section (p. 164) and eight expressions from the listening section (p. 166).

3. On each of the twenty slips of paper, the caller writes down a vocabulary term or expression from this section of the unit (see pages 164 and 166).

4. The caller places the twenty slips of paper in a hat.

5. The caller randomly selects a slip of paper from the hat and reads the vocabulary term aloud.

6. Players place a token on the corresponding vocabulary term in their grids.

7. Steps 5 and 6 are repeated until one of the players has placed four tokens in a row (horizontally, vertically or diagonally).

8. The first player to get four in a row says "Bingo" and wins the prize.

Suggestion: Repeat the activity; this time, the winning player has to explain the meaning of the four terms that gave him or her a "bingo" in order to collect the prize. If he or she can't correctly explain the terms, no prize is given and the game continues.

graduate	cover the cost	recall	leading cause
on religious grounds	outbreak	be underway	strike
flu shot	cripple	breathing	looming pandemic
spine	time slot	onset	virulent strain

Would You Like to Work Together?

In this section, you are asked to work with another student on a speaking project.

Project Overview

In the "Did You Know?" section of this part of the unit, you read a historical **overview** article about vaccination (pp. 157–158). One way to summarize an article and assimilate information is to write questions, the answers to which are found in the article you are reading. Take for example the first sentence of the "Did You Know?" article: "A vaccine is a preparation containing weakened or dead strains of a microbe that causes disease." A question you could write based on the information contained in this sentence would be, "What is a vaccine?" Working with a partner, you must create ten questions based on the "Did You Know?" article; then you must ask these questions to another team of two in the class.

Procedure
This activity is carried out in two parts.

Part A
1. Working with your chosen (or assigned) partner, create ten questions based on the "Did You Know?" article. Note: Use a combination of "yes/no" and "information questions." Use at least two different tenses when writing your questions. (To review question formation, see *Parallels: Exploring the Issues English Grammar*.) After each question, name the tense used (simple present, present continuous, simple past, past continuous, etc.)

double-check verify by checking a second time

2. **Double-check** your question formation and submit your list of questions to your teacher for verification.

Part B
3. With your partner, challenge another team of two to correctly respond to your teacher-verified list of questions. Note: You must read (not show) your questions to the opposing team and neither team may look back at the original article.

4. Give one point for each correct answer and zero points for each incorrect answer. If you're unsure about the answer, ask your teacher to act as "referee."

5. Alternate asking and answering questions with the other team.

6. The team with the highest score wins!

Variation: Your teacher may increase the difficulty of this project by selecting two new articles on vaccination and giving copies of the articles to all teams of two. All teams read both articles. Half of the teams write questions based on Article A, and half of the teams write questions based on Article B. The "challenge" is then carried out as described in Part B above, pairing Article A teams with Article B teams.

If I Did Wrong, the Other Person Was at Fault, Okay?

By Lisa Fitterman

Recently, my husband and I got up at the ungodly hour of 4 a.m. to catch an early flight to New York. We were preternaturally[1] calm, perhaps because we were sleepwalking. And we were all ready when the taxi came to collect us 45 minutes later.

It was an uneventful ride to the airport. We didn't even chat, because he was watching an episode of *24* on his new iPod. "Men and their toys," he said apologetically.

At the airport, the cabbie pulled in to let us off, at which point iPod guy turned to me, ashen-faced, and said: "We don't have our suit bag."

"You're joking, right?" I replied, for he always lies like that.

"No. I mean it. Did you bring down the suit bag? I didn't."

"What do you mean, you didn't bring down the suit bag?" I hissed. "All our stuff is in that suit bag. Your suit. Your shoes. My skirt."

You stupid jerk, I was thinking, you're always supposed to do things like bring down luggage. This is your fault and now we're going to miss our flight, miss the fabulous event we're supposed to be at tonight and miss New York altogether.

I didn't say that out loud, though. He already knew how I felt. Besides, I was travelling on his dime.

The entire episode showcased what I grudgingly admit is an unpleasant side to my personality, namely, that I have a hard time accepting responsibility, partial or otherwise. I know this because other people have pointed it out—repeatedly. They say I can be unfair, arrogant and selfish, even if I insist that blaming the other guy is really self-preservation.

Then again, we all tend to lie to ourselves and other people about our failings, don't we? Or, at least, gloss over them as if they don't mean a thing. If I cheat on my taxes, for example, doesn't everyone? Not—I repeat, not—that I'd ever cheat on my taxes.

But it's hard to look in a mirror and see a cheater, liar, gossip, or worse, a martyr who thinks she's always right, staring back at you. Unless, of course, she's always right.

But enough about me; what do you think of me? Psychologists posit that the best way to assess ourselves—our true selves—is through the eyes of others. They say that flawed and inflated self-assessment is as rife as, well, faults, and that the least competent people systematically misjudge and overestimate their abilities, which, in turn, can adversely affect key things in their lives such as health, relationships and finances.

We often don't (or won't) recognize when we've done wrong, and when we do, it's always the other person's fault. Like when I came home after practically totalling our car and told the husband that I'd been sideswiped by a cab, omitting the salient fact that I'd been in the process of making a U-turn to grab a parking spot on the other side of the street.

Or the classic (and perhaps apocryphal[2]) excuse on some motorist's accident form for his insurance company: "A pedestrian hit me and went under my car."

As David Myers, a professor at Hope College in Holland, Michigan, who wrote the textbook *Social Psychology*, told the *Seattle Times*, "Most of us have a good reputation with ourselves."

True enough, if you consider the classic study from 1977, when 94 percent of American college professors rated themselves as above average, even though only 50 percent could be in the top half in the first place. But that could also be characterized as willful ignorance.

On which count I plead guilty, your honour.

Oh, and that missing suit bag? We hightailed it home in the taxi, picked it up, returned to the airport and made it through with minutes to spare.

Later, while strolling along Broadway, I noted how proud I was I hadn't said a thing about him forgetting our clothes at home. He just smiled and shook his head.

679 words

---

1. preternaturally: a formal or literary term meaning "unnaturally"
2. apocryphal: a formal or literary term meaning "fictional"

Youth Gambling a Growing Concern

By Paul Barton

With many new television shows profiling high-stakes poker games, and with a range of Internet sites promoting poker and other gaming activity, it's no wonder gambling among teenagers has become increasingly popular.

The social acceptance of gambling in general is masking a growing problem with teenage gambling.

Various studies in Canada, the United States, Europe, Australia and New Zealand report an increase in both legal and illegal gambling among today's youth. Studies of adult gambling addicts found that in many instances, gambling behaviours began during teenage years, with some problem gamblers beginning the habit as young as 10.

About 80 percent of high school students have reported gambling for money at some point, according to a report published by McGill University. This report also outlined that among today's youth, 8 percent of teenagers have serious gambling problems and 15 percent of adolescents are at serious risk of developing troubling gambling habits.

The popularization and glamorizing of gambling has caused some teenagers to have an unrealistic understanding about gambling and the chances of success. One study found many teens believe they have a 50/50 chance of winning at games of chance or with lottery prizes when, in fact, the odds of winning are much less.

May Start Small

Gambling problems with an individual may start out small, but if the youth falls into debt over gambling, behavioural changes could surface.

Sometimes an unfavourable attitude and sudden behaviour changes displayed by some teenagers may be dismissed as the teenager going through puberty.

In such instances, the parent may unknowingly be overlooking a more serious underlying problem. If questioned, teenagers with gambling problems may quickly dismiss any notion that they have a problem.

Some of the signs your teenager may have a gambling problem are surprisingly similar to signs your teenager may have a drug or other substance-abuse problem. Clues to addictive problems in teenagers include:

- Disruption in family relationships—withdrawing from being a part of the family;

- Problems with peer relationships—suddenly hanging out with new friends and/or changing friends often;

- Decline in school and/or job performance—lack of focus and lack of motivation;

- Signs of low self-esteem and depression;

- Moodiness and poor sleep patterns.

Regarding addictive behaviour, one psychologist consulted on this topic suggests that often an underlying problem exists, and rather than deal with the underlying issue, the individual uses his or her "drug of choice" to escape problems.

Unless dealt with, the problems may worsen. At times, gambling problems can migrate to delinquent and criminal behaviour, such as stealing money or stealing property to sell for money to fuel gambling habits.

Like many things in life, moderation is the key. When gambling is taken to extreme levels, the addictive behaviours serious gamblers have are no less serious than any other addictive behaviours.

Ongoing Education

Given the long-term effects gambling could have on teenagers, ongoing education about the consequences of problem gambling is necessary to ensure they don't ruin their financial future by developing gambling habits early in life. Teens need to understand the potential negative implications gambling could have.

If you have children, what should you be talking to them about regarding gambling? Discussions about gambling could cover any number of points, such as talking about the low odds of winning on games of chance.

Real-life examples are another way to explain how gambling can lead to trouble. The Internet is full of stories of people that let gambling get out of hand, ultimately ruining their financial situation in the process.

Games of chance may provide an adrenaline rush and entertainment for some. However, remember that gambling is not a substitute for sound retirement planning.

618 words

Eating Fewer Calories Could Lead to Longer Life

By Lindsey Tanner

CHICAGO – Longevity researchers say they've shown for the first time that following a strict low-calorie diet can decrease DNA damage linked with aging.

Some people who took part in the six-month diet study ate as little as 890 calories a day. Their insulin levels fell and metabolisms slowed—changes that are thought to increase longevity.

The findings are provocative, but preliminary. Longer-term research will try to sort out whether such changes can meaningfully extend people's lives, said senior author Eric Ravussin of the Pennington Biomedical Research Center at Louisiana State University.

"They are the first proof that what has been observed in rodents seems to be also working in humans," Ravussin said.

The results are from the first phase of research at the Baton Rouge centre sponsored by a $12.4 million US National Institute on Aging (NIA) grant. They follow unrelated research reported in January, which suggested a very restrictive diet seemed to help the heart age more slowly.

The latest study appears in today's *Journal of the American Medical Association*.

"It's very exciting," said Dr. Evan Hadley, director of the NIA's geriatrics and clinical gerontology program.

"It's a step forward but not the whole journey," said Hadley, whose agency is part of the NIH.

The 48 participants, all slightly overweight, were randomly assigned to one of four groups: calorie restriction, which cut usual daily calories by 25 percent; calorie restriction plus exercise, which cut daily calories by 12.5 percent and increased physical activity by 12.5 percent five days a week; very low calories, with an 890-calorie liquid diet for up to about three months followed by a weight-maintenance diet; and a control group that aimed to keep weight steady.

Government dietary guidelines for weight maintenance recommend about 2,000 to 3,000 calories a day, depending on age, gender and activity level, with the higher amount generally for very active men.

The non-liquid diets used in the study were high in fruits and vegetables with less than 30 percent fat.

Average weight loss was about 18 pounds, slightly more in the liquid-diet group.

Blood tests showed substantial decreases in the amount of age-related DNA damage in each of the three dieting groups, compared with their initial levels. That kind of microscopic damage is linked to cancer and other age-related ailments, but it's unknown whether the small changes seen in the study would affect the study volunteers' disease risks.

No changes were seen in the control group.

Insulin levels also decreased after six months in all three reduced-calorie groups. Core body temperature also dipped slightly in two low-calorie groups but not in the liquid-diet or control group.

The results show that the diets are safe, and not impossible to follow, Hadley said.

464 words

On the Road

By Andrea Macko

One of the best things about the warm weather is the return to safer driving; no longer inhibited by snow, ice, or combinations thereof, motorists can tool about unencumbered by risks of poor road conditions.

If only it were that simple! St. Marys, so far, has escaped any truly horrendous pothole problems, but travellers to other cities know the season of "shock and awwww …" is upon us when it comes to their car axles. But there is a bigger problem on the roads, and it's the fault of humans. How many times have you been in a near-accident, only to peer closely at the instigator to realize that they are yakking away on a cellphone (or, for that matter, you were)? While a review of studies shows debate over a direct link between cellphone use and accident rates, it is agreed that using a cellphone while driving does distract drivers—just like the distractions of eating, changing CDs or disciplining rowdy children in the backseat.

There is a long list of countries that have banned cellphone use while driving, or limited usage to hands-free devices. In Canada, Newfoundland is the only province with a ban (since 2002). While other provinces have introduced legislation in the past, Quebec and Nova Scotia now have an all-out ban, and a limit to hands-free usage, respectively, on April 1 (no fooling).

There is much debate over their effectiveness. While many dislike being told what to do while inside their own vehicle, others, especially those in the medical field, believe that merely a hands-free line doesn't go far enough in cutting the driving distractions. The benefit of having a cellphone in a vehicle is great, especially in emergency situations—but surely, each call made or received while driving isn't about a flat tire or an accident. And then there is the enforcement issue; how to do so fairly and effectively? If you've ever used a cellphone while driving, you know it cuts down on reaction time and awareness. Dialing and driving is certainly a step up from walking and chewing gum, and hopefully many realize this and cut down calls, or at least wait until stopped or parked to do so.

But if you're still blissfully unaware of the risk while driving, consider this: A recent study from Carnegie Mellon University in Pittsburgh showed that listening to any noise while behind the wheel reduces 37 per cent of brain activity associated with driving. In the past, it was believed that since driving and talking skills come from different sections of the brain, people could handle it, but the results show otherwise. There is also the risk of offending who you're talking to while on your cell; since the brain is so busy operating your car and trying to converse, conversations may come across as rude and insulting, the study noted, adding a unique level of stress to the conversation.

Certainly, however, being rude to someone during a call while on the road isn't nearly as stressful as a car accident or the potential for injuries, fines or even death.

524 words

I'm as Sick as a Dog—Literally

By Don Braid

By about 10 a.m. Saturday, I realized that I was feeling about 90 percent human.

That's not bad for a newspaper columnist, you might say. It's certainly good for me after a three-week battle with influenza.

The flu has hit the city early and hard. Calgary Health Region (CHR) officials are exceptionally concerned. They're already facing evidence of an early onset of serious cases.

"Heading into flu season, we're seeing a higher volume of patients, and a higher volume of sicker patients," says CHR vice-president Don Campbell.

Emergency room visits are up 10 percent from last year. Sixteen percent of the patients are classified as serious, as opposed to 13 percent a year ago.

These are early signs that the flu could burst the system's seams if it gets out of hand.

If you catch this bug, you won't be thinking about the system; it's your own seams you'll be worried about.

The flu that levelled me, along with many other Calgarians, is A Fujian, a nasty respiratory illness that digs into the chest within hours, quickly causing bronchitis and even pneumonia.

It made me as sick as I've been in twenty years, but here's the thing—I probably escaped the full force of this illness.

A few weeks before coming down with it, I had this year's flu shot. It protects against another strain, A Panama, which apparently is less serious than our surprise early visitor.

But experts say the A Panama vaccine provides "crossover" protection against A Fujian. If you're vaccinated but still catch the flu, chances are your symptoms will be milder.

If my flu was an easy version of A Fujian, I am darned happy I didn't catch the whole thing.

Bronchitis hit within days and everything got worse from there—extreme weakness, chills, headache and an insane cough that went on for hours, especially at night.

Banished to the basement so the rest of the family could get some sleep, I often ended up on my hands and knees, barking like my old dog Blue.

Except that I wasn't chasing squirrels, and the bark wouldn't stop. Even the strongest codeine cough medicine didn't touch that cough.

This flu is sneaky, too; it seems to ease after two weeks, and then comes back like a freight train.

There's a simple message here: get a vaccination, and have your kids vaccinated too.

We don't usually vaccinate children against flu, but this illness has already killed susceptible youngsters in the US. The need to vaccinate all seniors couldn't be more obvious.

The CHR is aggressively trying to get that done, partly through its excellent partnership with Co-op stores. Thirty-nine thousand people have already been vaccinated at stores, 6,000 more than last year.

On the national level, there's talk of stockpiling antiviral drugs and creating "fever hospitals" to treat influenza patients outside regular hospitals, in an effort to keep the flu from spreading.

All this sounds theoretical until you get sick. Then it becomes extremely personal.

A nurse at a family clinic told me Friday that some young mothers are so ill they literally can't get out of bed to look after their toddlers. Whole families have been levelled for days or even weeks.

So please take this advice from a re-emerging human: get the flu shot.

556 words

The Persuasive Essay

In the persuasive essay, the writer attempts to persuade readers that his or her opinion on a controversial subject is the right one. The writer presents one side of the controversy and supports his or her opinion with two arguments, each of which is supported by a statistic, an example or an expert opinion. In short 200- to 250-word essays, writing four paragraphs is standard practice.

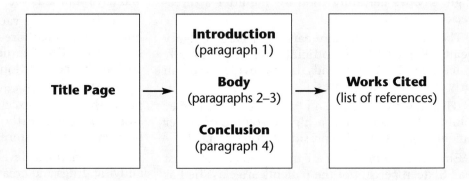

Introduction

The first paragraph of a persuasive essay is called the introduction.

The introduction begins with a *grabber*, a technique used to grab (or capture) the reader's attention. Effective grabber techniques for essays include:

1. **Quotations**
   American playwright Wilson Mizner once said that gambling is "the sure way of getting nothing for something."

2. **Definitions**
   "Risking money or valuables in hopes of winning more than you're risking is gambling."

3. **Facts**
   Approximately two percent of Canadian adults experience gambling problems.

The introduction ends with a thesis statement, an affirmative sentence that expresses the writer's opinion about the subject of the essay.

For example: *Gambling is a dangerous game.*

Development

The second and third paragraphs are called the development.

The first sentence of each of these paragraphs begins with a transition term (*First, Second/To begin, To continue*) followed by an argument in support of the thesis statement. The first sentence (also called the topic sentence) must be backed up with some form of evidence.

There are three types of evidence:

1. **Statistics**
   Facts: *In Canada, gambling falls under the jurisdiction of the provincial government.*
   Figures: *In 2001, Canadian lotteries generated 3.5 billion dollars in revenue.*

2. **Expert Opinion**
   Quote: *Public health expert Jeffrey Marotta believes that "… gambling on campus is risky business."*
   Paraphrase: *Public health expert Jeffrey Marotta believes that campus gambling is risky.*

3. **Example**
   Phyllis Vineberg's son committed suicide due to a gambling addiction.

Two different types of evidence are used in the development.

Conclusion

The fourth paragraph is called the conclusion.

The conclusion begins with a transition term (*In summary/To conclude*) and a summary: the thesis and the two arguments are restated.

The essay ends with a *clincher*, a technique used to encourage the reader to think about the essay. Clincher techniques include:

1. **Connecting with the Introduction**
   An example of connecting to Grabber Technique #1 (see "Introduction" on page 178) would be: *So Wilson Mizner was right: gambling takes a lot—and gives very little in return.*

2. **Rhetorical Question**
   Is gambling a dangerous pastime? For most of us, no. But for a significant minority, it is not only dangerous—it is life-threatening.

3. **Offering a Suggestion**
   The government should close down casinos and open up community centres where citizens can enrich their lives—and not government coffers.

Citation Style

Before writing a persuasive essay, you must do some research. Any research referred to in your essay must be correctly cited.

When you quote (use somebody's exact words), paraphrase (rephrase somebody's words) or refer to another writer's work, you must reference the writer to avoid being accused of plagiarism.

There are many different citation styles. The style suggested in this textbook is adapted from the *Modern Language Association (MLA) Citation Style*.

Basically, a citation has two interrelated parts:

1. **Parenthetical Reference**

2. **Works-Cited List**

The parenthetical reference is in the body of the essay and the works-cited list appears at the end of the essay.

Parenthetical Reference

Parenthetical references are essential for quotes and paraphrases. Print sources (newspapers, books) and Internet sources are cited differently.

If the author of your quote or paraphrase is cited in someone else's work, use the term "as cited in." For example: (Willsey, as cited in Little 25). In this case, a complete reference to Little should appear in the works-cited list. Remember: If an organization writes an article, the organization is considered to be the author.

Source	Author's Name Is Mentioned in the Reference	Author's Name Is Not Mentioned in the Reference
Print	Parenthetical references should include the **page number**. *Doug Little wrote, "I am gambling my life away." (2)*	Parenthetical references should include the **author's last name** and the **page number**. *One problem gambler stated, "I am gambling my life away." (Little 2)*
Internet	No parenthetical reference is required. *Diana Swift maintains that for problem gamblers, "… gambling is no longer a game, but a compulsion. They can't stop, and they can't control when and how long they play or how much they spend."*	Parenthetical references should include the **author's last name**. *For problem gamblers, "… gambling is no longer a game, but a compulsion. They can't stop, and they can't control when and how long they play or how much they spend." (Swift)*

Works Cited

On a separate page at the end of your essay, you must list all sources paraphrased or quoted. Follow these guidelines:

- The sources are in alphabetical order by last name (or by organization or by title if no author has been identified).
- *Italicize* or <u>underline</u> all titles of complete works (newspapers, books, TV series, etc.).
- Use quotation marks for titles of works contained in another work (articles, book chapters, TV episodes, etc.).
- Capitalize all important words in a title.
- If using an Internet source, indicate the date accessed using the form "day/month/year."
- All entries are double-spaced, and the second (and third and fourth) lines of each entry are indented (as are the second, third and fourth paragraphs of the essay).

The following lists common types of sources accompanied by examples. In particular, notice how Little's and Swift's works (see Parenthetical Reference examples on page 180) are cited.

Type of Source	Example
1. Book with one author	Little, Doug. *Losing Mariposa: The Memoir of a Compulsive Gambler.* Toronto: ECW Press, 2002.
2. Article in a newspaper or magazine.	Williams, Brian. "Bad Poker Night Curbed My Enthusiasm." *Guelph Mercury*: 1 December 2006: A2.
3. Article on a website	Swift, Diana. "Conquer a Gambling Addiction." *Homemakers.com*. Retrieved: 14 January 2008. http://www.homemakers.com/Health/healthymind/conquer-a-gambling-addiction-n234334p1.html
4. Website	*Stop Gambling.* "21 Steps to Stop Gambling." Retrieved: 19 January 2008. http://21stepstostopgambling.com/index.html

The Title Page

An academic institution often has its own unique title-page requirements. In general, a title page should contain the following elements:

1. **Essay Title**
   An abbreviated thesis statement is often a good title.

2. **Student's Name**
   Use first and last names.

3. **Teacher's Name**
   Don't forget courtesy titles such as Mr., Mrs., Ms. or Dr.

4. **Course Title**
   Indicate course code, if any.

5. **Academic Institution**
   Use the complete name of your school.

6. **Date Submitted**
   Make sure your assignment is on time!

In some cases, the instructor may also require that you indicate the word count. If this is the case, do not count words in quotations.

Notice that in the example title page (p. 183), the first four elements are centred in the top third of the page, and the last two elements are centred in the bottom third of the page.

The title page (and the entire essay) should be double-spaced with 2.54-cm margins to allow room for correction.

Example Persuasive Essay

Read the annotated persuasive essay on the subject of gambling (pp. 183–186). Following the essay, you will find information on persuasive strategies and language structures. **Note:** Double-space essays and indent the developing and concluding paragraphs.

Gambling Is a Dangerous Game

By
(Student's name)

Presented to
(Teacher's name)

For the course
(Course name and code)

(Academic institution)

(Date submitted)

Grabber (Quotation)	American playwright Wilson Mizner once said that gambling is, "The sure way of getting nothing for something." (as cited on famous-quotations.com) Players risk their hard-earned dollars for the chance of winning large sums of money; however, most walk away losers—not winners—as the odds are stacked against the players from the very start. To put it bluntly, gambling is a loser's game. Gambling is also a very dangerous game.
Thesis statement (Opinion on gambling)	
First transition term and argument (Topic sentence 1)	First, Statistics Canada estimates that problem gamblers make up 0.6 percent of the Canadian population (as cited on *CBC News*). At first glance, 0.6 percent of the Canadian population may seem insignificant; however, this percentage represents almost 200,000 Canadians—200,000 Canadians who have a serious problem that threatens their physical, emotional and financial well-being, not to mention the well-being of their loved ones.
Evidence (Statistics)	
Second transition term and argument (Topic sentence 2)	Second, The Canada Safety Council believes that more than 200 problem gamblers commit suicide every year and that more than 1,000 are hospitalized with self-inflicted injuries. Phyllis Vineberg can speak about gambling-related suicides from personal experience: her son Trevor took his life as a result of a gambling addiction when he was only twenty-five years old. Since Trevor's death, Ms. Vineberg has crusaded to have video lottery terminals (VLTs) removed from school
Evidence (Statistic and anecdote)	

zones so that what happened to her family won't happen to other families (*CTV News*).

Transition term and summary

Clincher (connecting with the Introduction)

To conclude, gambling is dangerous because it threatens the well-being of nearly 200,000 Canadians and takes more than 200 lives every year. Perhaps Mr. Mizner wasn't completely correct. Gambling does give gamblers something: an impoverished and shortened life.

Note 1
The list is titled.

Note 2
The works are listed
in alphabetical order
by last name.

Note 3
The entries are
double-spaced.

Note 4
For each work cited,
indent all lines but
the first.

Works Cited

Canada Safety Council. "Canadian Roulette." Retrieved:

14 January 2008.

http://www.safety-council.org/info/community/gambling.html

CBC News. "Betting the Farm: an Overview of Gambling Addiction."

Retrieved: 24 July 2007.

http://www.cbc.ca/news/background/gambling/addiction.html

CTV News. "Teen Gambling." CTV, Toronto. 16 May 2005.

Famous Quotations Network. Ed. Haythum R. Khalid.

"Categories: Miscellaneous." Retrieved: 15 January 2008.

http://www.famous-quotations.com/asp/search.asp?keyword=

gambling&Submit=Find

Persuasive Strategies

Here are two strategies to use when writing a persuasive essay:

1. **Don't use any first or second person pronouns (*I, you, we; my, your, our;* etc.)**
   By only using the third person singular or plural (*he, she, it; they*), the essay appears impersonal and rational.

2. **Don't use any contractions (*he's, they're, we're,* etc.) unless your teacher indicates otherwise.**
   Using a formal writing style will lend credibility to your essay.

Transition Terms

A list of some commonly used transition terms and the functions of these terms is included below.

Function	Examples
to add an idea	*also, in addition (to), furthermore, moreover*
to emphasize an idea	*indeed, in fact*
to provide an example	*for example, for instance, to illustrate*
to show a result	*therefore, as a result*
to show a contrast	*however, nevertheless, otherwise, on the other hand*
to conclude	*to conclude, in conclusion, in summary, in brief, briefly*

Discourse and Debate

Discourse

A persuasive discourse is a formal public speech intended to persuade listeners that the speaker's opinion on a controversial subject is the right one. Like the persuasive essay (see "Appendix A"), one side of the controversy is presented and the speaker's opinion is supported with arguments backed up by statistics, examples and expert opinions. In short three- to four-minute speeches, presenting two arguments is standard practice.

The structure of a persuasive discourse is similar to that of a persuasive essay: an introduction, a development and a conclusion are required.

Introduction

Like the persuasive essay, the persuasive speech begins with a grabber, which is a technique used to grab (or capture) the listener's attention. Effective grabber techniques for public speaking include:

1. **Rhetorical Questions**
   Do you want to look your best? Of course you do.

2. **Provocative Statements**
   How you look is more important than who you are!

3. **Short Anecdotes**
   A Montreal newspaper recently sent two reporters to apply for a job selling beauty products: one was an attractive twenty-one-year-old with no retail experience, and the other was a rather plain-looking forty-seven-year-old with more than ten years experience selling cosmetics. It should come as no surprise to learn that …

At the end of the introduction, the speaker provides a preview statement, an affirmative sentence that expresses the speaker's opinion (the thesis statement) and enumerates the two arguments the speaker will present to support his or her opinion.

For example: *Discriminating against people on the basis of their appearance is wrong for two reasons. First, inner beauty is more important than outer beauty. Second, physical beauty is in the eye of the beholder.*

Development

In the development, the speaker's two arguments are developed. Each argument is introduced with a transition term (*To begin/To Continue*) and must be supported with **at least two** of the following three types of evidence:

1. **Statistics**
   In 2003, more than three million Botox treatments were carried out in the United States.

2. **Expert Opinion**
   According to Dr. Jane Smith, Botox treatment ...

3. **Example**
   Robert Lyon had his first Botox treatment at the age of twenty-eight. He ...

Conclusion

The conclusion begins with a transition term (*To conclude/In summary*) and a summary statement, a rephrased preview statement (see "Introduction" on page 188). The speaker ends with a clincher, which is a technique used to encourage the listener to think about what the speaker has said. Effective clincher techniques for public speaking include:

1. **Connecting with the Introduction**
   An example of connecting to Grabber Technique #1 (see "Introduction" on page 188) would be: *So you want to look your best? Forget about plastic surgery: eat right, exercise daily and laugh every chance you get.*

2. **Demonstrating the Importance of the Thesis Statement**
   If people fully understood the risks associated with plastic surgery, they would never "go under the knife."

3. **Offering a Solution**
   The next time you notice those laugh lines around your eyes, remember that they are badges of honour—signs of a life well lived.

Persuasive Strategies

There are four basic rules to keep in mind when giving a persuasive discourse:

1. **Keep it short and simple.**
   Your sentences should be short and your language should be simple.

2. **Repeat yourself.**
   While readers can go back and reread, an audience cannot go back and "re-listen." Don't be afraid to repeat key pieces of information to help your listeners follow along.

3. Use transition terms.

Transition words like "first, second" and "to begin, to continue" are essential in order to help your listeners follow your train of thought. (See examples of common transition terms on page 193.)

4. Ask questions.

There are two types of questions that you should ask: rhetorical (questions that don't require responses from the audience as you both ask and answer the questions) and directed (you select members of the audience and ask them questions). Never direct a question to a group of people. More often than not, no one will respond.

A Few Don'ts

Here are a few things not to do when giving a speech.

- Don't read your speech.
- Don't stand in one place.
- Don't talk to just one or two people in the audience.
- Don't avoid making eye contact.

Practise your speech ahead of time so that you don't feel the need to read it. It's a good idea to move about and "connect" with all members of the audience. As the saying goes, "You can't trust someone who doesn't look you in the eye." Let your audience know they can trust you—and what you have to say!

Debate

A debate is a structured public discussion in which two teams take opposing positions on a controversial proposition. There are ten propositions suggested as class debates in this textbook:

1. Gun registration is wrong.
   (Unit 2, Section A)

2. Actions to stop global warming are wrong.
   (Unit 2, Section B)

3. A prohibition on gambling is wrong.
   (Unit 3, Section A)

4. Physical enhancement through plastic surgery is wrong.
   (Unit 3, Section B)

5. Adopting a simple-living lifestyle is wrong.
   (Unit 4, Section A)

6. Adopting a caloric restriction lifestyle is wrong.
   (Unit 4, Section B)

7. Restricting juvenile cellphone usage is wrong.
   (Unit 5, Section A)

8. Eugenic interventions are wrong.
   (Unit 5, Section B)

9. Current public-security measures are wrong.
   (Unit 6, Section A)

10. Mandatory vaccination is wrong.
    (Unit 6, Section B)

In the "Did You Know" sections of each unit, two arguments are suggested "for" and two arguments "against" each of these ten propositions.

The team in favour of the proposition is referred to as the **affirmative team**, and the team opposed to the proposition is referred to as the **negative team**. Each team is composed of two students, and there are two speeches:

1. The First Speech

2. The Second Speech

The affirmative team begins the debate, and the negative team ends the debate.

Overview of the Debate

The schema below shows the speaking order in a debate. The affirmative team begins, the negative team continues, the affirmative team responds and the negative team ends.

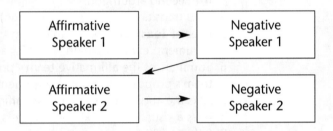

Overview of the Speeches

The first and second speeches are **one formal speech given by two people**. Like the four-paragraph persuasive essay, the speech is based on a thesis supported by two arguments. The first speaker does the introduction and explains the first argument. The second speaker presents the second argument and does the conclusion.

Debating Suggestion: Have a moderator for the debate. He/She introduces the debate, ensures that speakers respect their time and asks the audience to indicate the winning team by a show of hands.

Structure of the Affirmative Speeches

The debate is a highly structured oral presentation. Each speaker has certain tasks to perform in order to respect the structure. The chart on page 192 outlines the tasks for each speaker.

Affirmative Speakers	Tasks
First	1. Introduces the team and greets the audience. 2. Captures the audience's attention with an anecdote, a question, etc. 3. States the subject of the debate and the affirmative team's proposition. 4. Indicates the two arguments to be used to support the proposition and develops the first argument. 5. Uses transition words (see next page). 6. Uses **at least two** of the following types of evidence to support the first argument: expert opinion, statistics and example. 7. Summarizes the argument and reminds the audience of the one remaining argument to be presented by the second speaker. 8. Uses a visual aid (blackboard, posters, handouts, etc.). 9. Refers to, but does not read, notes. 10. Respects speaking time (three to four minutes).
Second	1. Introduces self. 2. Politely criticizes something the first negative speaker said or did. 3. Reminds the audience of the affirmative team's first argument and presents the second argument. 4. Uses transition words (see next page). 5. Uses **at least two** of the following types of evidence to support the second argument: expert opinion, statistics and example. 6. Summarizes the affirmative team's position, reminding the audience of the team's proposition and two arguments. 7. Asks the audience to support the affirmative team's position. 8. Uses a visual aid (blackboard, posters, handouts, etc.). 9. Refers to, but does not read, notes. 10. Respects speaking time (three to four minutes).

Structure of the Negative Speeches

The debate is a highly structured oral presentation. Each speaker has certain tasks to perform in order to respect the structure. The chart below outlines the tasks for each speaker.

Negative Speakers	Tasks
First	1. Introduces the team and greets the audience. 2. Politely criticizes something the first affirmative speaker said or did. 3. States the negative team's opposition to the affirmative proposition. 4. Indicates the two arguments to be used to support the negative team's opposition. 5. Uses transition words (see next page). 6. Uses **at least two** of the following types of evidence to support the first argument: expert opinion, statistics and example. 7. Summarizes the argument and reminds the audience of the remaining argument to be presented by the second speaker. 8. Uses a visual aid (blackboard, posters, handouts, etc.). 9. Refers to, but does not read, notes. 10. Respects speaking time (three to four minutes).

Negative Speakers	Tasks
Second	1. Introduces self. 2. Politely criticizes something the second affirmative speaker said or did. 3. Reminds the audience of the negative team's first argument and presents the second argument. 4. Uses transition words (see next page). 5. Uses **at least two** of the following types of evidence to support the second argument: expert opinion, statistics and example. 6. Summarizes the negative team's position, reminding the audience of the team's opposition and two arguments. 7. Asks the audience to support the negative team's position. 8. Uses a visual aid (blackboard, posters, handouts, etc.). 9. Refers to, but does not read, notes. 10. Respects speaking time (three to four minutes).

Transition Terms

The following is a list of common transition terms useful in debating.

Function	Examples
to add an idea	*also, what's more, in addition, to add to that*
to conclude	*to finish up, to wrap up, to conclude*
to emphasize an idea	*I repeat, as I said*
to provide an example	*for example, to illustrate*
to sequence	*first, second*
to show a contrast	*on the one hand … on the other hand, on the contrary*
to show a result	*because of this, as a result*

NOTES